THE LIFE OF
RADCLYFFE HALL

Radclyffe Hall and Una Troubridge in Edy Craig's
Garden at Smallhythe 1931.

THE LIFE
OF
RADCLYFFE HALL

by

Una, Lady Troubridge

The Citadel Press

New York

FIRST AMERICAN EDITION 1963
MANUFACTURED IN THE UNITED STATES OF AMERICA
PUBLISHED BY THE CITADEL PRESS
222 PARK AVENUE SOUTH, NEW YORK 3

LIBRARY OF CONGRESS CATALOG CARD NUMBER 63-11768

Foreword

A number of people have asked me to write all that I know of John, of her life both before and since I shared it. They have warned me that if I die leaving it unwritten many things that her readers will want to know, will have the right to know, about a writer of her talent, will be buried with me.

I have hesitated: an expurgated biography is of no value to anyone, an idealized biography would be an insult to her honesty and sincerity, but a perfectly truthful biography must of necessity involve others and include indiscretions of which she, with her high code of honour, might disapprove. But after all, she herself always dwelt of choice in the palace of truth, where I dwelt with her, and I have decided, so far as in me lies, to tell the truth, the whole truth and nothing but the truth. As I am no scribe, except that I am much addicted to letter-writing, I have decided to write all I know of John in the form of a long letter addressed to those who will read it. Here then is 'The Life and Death of Radclyffe Hall'. . . .

Una Vincenzo Troubridge

Salvation

I will be full, oh, full of praise
For each and every nation.
I'll bless the Lord and all His ways,
And magnify Him all my days
As part of His Creation.
I'll have a band, a mighty band,
And no more idle strumming
When I go out to Jericho,
Across the plains to Jericho,
In the good time that's coming!

I will be bold and unafraid
And great with high endeavour;
And all the trumpets men have made,
And all the drums that men have played,
They shall be mine for ever.
There'll be a noise, a mighty noise
Of bugling and drumming
When I go out to Jericho,
Across the plains to Jericho,
In the good time that's coming!

So I'll be silent for a while,
And keep my soul from doubting.
There shall not be so long a mile
But I will foot it with a smile,
For some day I'll be shouting.
There'll be a shout, a mighty shout
To set the planets humming
When I go into Jericho,
Between the gates of Jericho,
In the good time that's coming!

Radclyffe Hall

I SUPPOSE I ought to begin this narrative with some account of John's origins and forebears, but I have no intention, for the present at any rate, of delving among records and pedigrees. For the purpose of these memories it seems to me sufficient to give a general idea of the very mixed strains that went to her making and to mention those few ancestors who are of general interest, even such as are only collaterally involved.

Her family crest, the Talbot's head, makes its first appearance, so far as I know, in the churchyard of Stratford-on-Avon, on the tomb of Dr. John Hall, who lived at the beautiful half-timbered house, 'Hall's Croft', in that town and married Susanna, daughter of William Shakespeare. They had, however, no male issue, and the descent is not in the direct line. Of the Halls, the earliest portrait known to me is that of the Reverend Samuel Hall who was, I believe, rather a remarkable man and was tutor to De Quincey of *Opium Eater* Fame. I possess also a portrait of his son, John Hall, a fair gentleman with handsome, clear-cut features and a fierce expression whose resemblance to his great-grand-daughter in a bad temper is quite remarkable! He was the father of Dr. Charles Radclyffe-Hall, whose portrait is also in my possession.

John Hall's mother was Sarah Radclyffe and, for reasons unknown to me but probably connected with some inheritance, he assumed her surname in addition to his own. Her portrait (family tradition called it a Lely which, though a

7

very fine picture, it certainly is not. In my opinion it is suggestive of Allan Ramsay) is of interest, apart from its artistic merit, as it was she who brought into John's bloodstream that of the Earls of Derwentwater, of the two Radclyffes who were beheaded for their support of James and of Charles Edward Stuart, and who in their turn were descended from Charles II, through the actress Moll Davis. One of these Earls of Derwentwater was not only a Jacobite patriot, but a poet and mystic. He was an ardent Catholic; miracles were said to have occurred at his tomb. There was even talk of a process for canonization and, more popularly, his name became associated with a natural phenomenon occurring over Derwentwater and known as the 'Derwentwater lights'. This, I think, exhausts practically all that I know of John's paternal descent until we come to her grandfather. I possess other pictures and some miniatures and silhouettes: portraits of John Hall's wife and sister-in-law, a rather fine painting of an elderly, jolly-looking divine in bands and a wig like Dr. Johnson's, known to John only as 'Uncle Shrigley', but he must have been at least a three times 'great' uncle. In any case I know of nothing connected with these people that throws any light upon the character and career of their last descendant; peace be to their ashes. . . .

On her mother's side she was American, her mother being Mary Jane Diehl of Philadelphia. Of her forebears I know very little beyond the fact that they hailed partly from Dutch emigrant stock (hence the name Diehl), were connected with Livingstones, of Scottish origin (but this I vaguely fancy was only by recent marriage) and, a detail which John always related with jeering laughter, were among the legion that claimed to have in their veins the blood of Pocahontas!

In this last connexion, however, there is something not uninteresting to be said. In spite of her blue eyes and fair colouring, there was about the construction of John's face and features something distinctly reminiscent of the North American Indian, and on one occasion when I persuaded her to colour her skin and go to a fancy-dress party in the costume of a brave, wearing the war bonnet, the effect was very surprising. After a good deal of protest she consented to being photographed in the costume and the photograph furnishes, I think, strong evidence in favour of my statement. Since her death, seeing for the first time photographs of the North American half-breed, Grey Owl, it struck me at once that he might have easily passed as her brother! In any case, whether she had a distant Indian strain or not, there was plenty of Celtic blood in her maternal ancestry to account for her creative imagination. There was even some Welsh blood, she told me, though I don't know how or where that came in. And so she was a compound of many races: North Country English, American, Scottish, Dutch, Welsh and, if we admit of legend and delve into history, American Indian via Pocahontas and French and Italian via Charles II!

John's own father, Radclyffe Radclyffe-Hall, was the only son of Dr. Charles Radclyffe-Hall, himself a son of the fierce-looking John Hall and an eminent physician who specialized in tuberculosis and (as we would now think, most unwisely) popularized Torquay as a resort for consumption. Beyond the fact that Dr. Radclyffe-Hall was an intimate friend of Bulwer Lytton, I know very little about him except that he lost, soon after his marriage, a beautiful step-daughter whom he had loved so devotedly that he mourned her for the rest of his life. He seems to have compelled his household to share this mourning, and to have banished

9

from his home all normal frivolities; he certainly would appear, like his granddaughter, to have had deep affections.

Of her father, John knew a little by hearsay and even less by personal memory, her mother having divorced him when she, John, was only three years old. She has told me that in her opinion the enforced gloom of his home and undue severity on the part of his father must have contributed to his early-developed insubordination and subsequent dissipation. His ex-tutor, by name Begley, was John's chief informant regarding her father when she grew to maturity and I think the picture was further filled in by her mother's implacable and indelible animosity.

John learned and told me that her father's childhood and adolescence were punctuated by scenes and disagreement with his father. Mr. Begley, however, had loved him dearly, and a personality by no means unlovable emerges from his narrative.

Radclyffe Radclyffe-Hall (as I know by photographs which show a very strong resemblance to his daughter) was extremely handsome. Blue-eyed, fair, not tall but well-built, with beautiful hands and feet. He adored animals, was a fine horseman and was always surrounded by dogs, especially poodles, which he is said to have trained to an almost incredible degree of understanding and behaviour. He claimed that one of his poodles, in an emergency, could and did make use of a chamber pot! – and there is a suggestion here that he had a sense of humour. He also loved the sea and in later life lived much aboard a small yacht. He had some talent for both music and painting, but seems to have lacked industry or perseverance in any direction. Such of his paintings as I have seen were definitely poor in quality, and, at any rate after his father's death, he was a rich man and earning was no inducement to industry. So far as John knew he never showed any talent for writing, either in prose or verse, and there is no evidence of such talent having existed in any of her forebears.

He seems to have scrambled through Eton and Oxford. I think he was at St. John's – and there is a record of his reading for the Bar – he told Begley that the 'dinners' gave him indigestion. He finally broke with his father and left Torquay in circumstances connected with a scandalous liaison with a fisherman's daughter. John knew her name and told it to me, but I have forgotten it, which is perhaps just as well! He certainly visited Torquay on at least one subsequent occasion. Having joined a theatrical touring company he arranged to make his appearance in his natal city as Charles Surface in 'The School for Scandal', an exploit, according to Begley, devised with the deliberate intention of enraging his father and creating a scandal in Torquay for that eminently conventional and respectable specialist. I possess a very attractive cabinet photograph of Radclyffe Radclyffe-Hall in this rôle.

John gathered, also from Begley, that he was of a markedly moody nature, subject to extreme variations of high spirits and depression, and that when he became a victim of melancholy he would either go off to his yacht and the sea that he loved, or even more often set out alone on a riding tour, with no definite goal, putting himself and his horse up at any country inn where accommodation was available, when rest became imperative for man and beast, and disappearing until such time as his mood passed and he chose to be heard of again.

His temper is said to have been quite uncontrollably violent (a temper inherited by his daughter who, however, learned to control it), and one of Begley's anecdotes related to his throwing a table-knife at a young woman who was temporarily under his 'protection' and who had disagreed with him in the course of a meal. The knife, fortunately, only pinned a fold of her dress to her chair.

And there the curtain – so far as my memory serves – comes down on the anecdotes related by Begley concerning his friend and pupil, 'Rat'. No; there is one more glimpse: a leg of mutton that, being either under- or over-cooked, failed to give satisfaction and was thrown down the kitchen stairs at the cook's head. . . .

As for John's personal memories of this author of her being, they are fragmentary and one of them at least is not, I think, to his credit as the father of an only and very delicate child. She remembers him, when she was very small, coming on horseback to see her at the house where she lived with her mother and her maternal grandmother, and his horse being held outside the door. Very clearly, being even at that age passionately interested in horses, she re-members the promise of a cream-coloured pony for which she waited and waited and waited, and which never materia-lized.

Subsequent meetings (her grandmother would periodi-cally take her to see him) seem to have left little or no impression until the last time she saw him, when she was eighteen years of age, on the eve of his departure for Cannes where he fell ill and was brought back to England in a dying condition. She told me that when she saw him he was emaciated and looked terribly ill and that she re-marked on this and upon his shattering cough. He replied that it was only his asthma and that it would improve when he got to the Riviera. He also remarked that he had not realized that he had such a good-looking daughter, seemed moved to a measure of interest and affection and told her he intended making a new will in which he would bequeath to her that part of his estate that was not already entailed upon her. He inquired about her studies and her aims in life and urged her to stick to one thing and not to be 'a Jack-of-all-trades as I have been' . . .

She felt affectionate and tearful, and was worried about his obvious depression and ill health. She never saw him again.

On the arrival of his yacht at Cannes, accompanied by his valet and his 'innamorata' of the moment, he was taken ashore desperately ill and the doctor when summoned informed these rather inadequate attendants that if they wished him to die in his own country no time must be lost. He was still alive when he reached England but died at the Lord Warden Hotel in Dover almost immediately after his arrival . . . John said, of tuberculosis, but there is no evidence of the fact so far as I know and it may have been pneumonia as something was said of a bitterly cold wind at Cannes . . . on the other hand, many years later, John's Italian doctors, investigating the original cause of the acute pulmonary tuberculosis from which she had suffered in adolescence, advanced the hypothesis that she might have taken the infection during that final visit to her father.

The new will had not been made, but the old one revealed a bequest for the benefit of a natural child, the daughter of a woman in humble circumstances: this child received an adequate income which one feels represented some sense of responsibility.

Her mother . . . Here the narrative could be lengthy, the data are only too abundant but they are not pleasant writing or reading. She had been married before, in America, and John's father was her second husband. I have always felt that the dissipated, irresponsible and neglectful 'Rat' was one hundred per cent the better parent.

At the age of three John was handed over unconditionally (with a very large annual allowance for maintenance and education) to a technically blameless mother who had not wanted a child (especially by a man whom she, after a brief infatuation, had grown to detest), and who had vainly tried every expedient to defeat gestation. John was her second child; an earlier baby, a girl named Florence, had died in infancy. From the hour of birth she disliked her second daughter, and later would frequently remark distastefully to the girl herself upon her resemblances to her father: 'Your hands are just like Radclyffe's'; 'You're the image of your father' . . . In the mother there was a violence of temper equal to that of the father, but unaccompanied by intellect or talent of any description. A brainless, vain, selfish woman, possessed of an unlimited obstinacy and of a certain shrewdness in compassing her aims. It is not pleasant to think of her as the guardian of an ailing and intensely sensitive child, whose only protection was an ageing grandmother who loved her but was too weak and too much intimidated by bullying and by actual violence, to protect her. An early champion, her nurse, known and beloved as 'M'Nana' was very soon dealt with by Mrs. Radclyffe-Hall. This nurse, finding on the child's body the marks of cruel beatings, protested that it was one thing to punish a child but a scandal to reduce it to such a condition . . . and was summarily dismissed. This story rests, I imagine, partly upon the child's own memory of beatings administered in accesses of fury and partly upon what John learned later from her grandmother to whom she afforded a refuge when she herself, on coming of age, left her mother's house.

Other memories: a governess known as 'Nottie' who seems to have been quite kind. A pug, her first dog, called

14

Joey, whom she loved and plagued and who loved her but never hesitated to bite her when annoyed. A poodle called Adolfe who was run over. An Airedale, Yoi, who seems to have survived quite a long time and who was terribly seasick on a steamer trip from Ilfracombe to Lynton . . . always animals, always beloved, and in that connection another miserable little incident.

The child, about eleven years old, travelling now with Nottie, with her mother and with her mother's singing-master and third husband, Alberto Visetti, and taking with them the child's adored canary, Pippin, cherished and finger-tame. At some hotel in Belgium, Signor Visetti suddenly decided that the canary and its cage were an encumbrance and decreed that the bird must be given to one of the waiters in the hotel . . . It would seem that neither mother, grandmother nor governess had the imagination or the pluck to oppose this decree, and so the party moved on, minus the canary. The child, suffering by that time from asthma that kept her sitting up awake night after night, and precluded by day from all playing or exercise, had plenty of time in which to meditate upon the possible vicissitudes of her beloved canary in unknown hands. . . . To the end of her days she never forgot the misery of leaving the canary unprotected among strangers. Even at that early age, such an incident struck at one of her most deeply-rooted instincts: that of protection towards anything weak or helpless . . . it grew to be in her case an all-pervading passion. And in this conjunction comes a memory connected with her grandmother from whom she herself learned of it. That as a very little girl indeed when crossing London streets she would put her hand on the elderly lady's arm and say: 'Hold on to me, granny, and I'll take you across. Don't be afraid . . .'

John was in her thirties when I got to know her first, and I in my twenties, sufficiently callous easily to lose patience and to say to her on one occasion: 'The trouble with you is that you've got protection mania. . . .' It was a mania that grew with the years, thank God, and flowered in every book she wrote and in her every thought and act to man and beast.

There is a pathetic photograph of her which I have often examined in the past. A faded shiny carte-de-visite obviously taken to exploit the 'paternal' affection of Alberto Visetti. John, a very thin, bony little girl of about ten, very unbecomingly dressed and with all the appearance of an unloved child, standing awkwardly beside the seated Visetti, already getting rather portly, the epitome of smug self-satisfaction and conceit.

His marriage to her mother, even apart from such incidents as I have already mentioned, was a disastrous affair for John . . . indeed the disadvantages latent in her mother's acquaintance with him began before their marriage took place. Presumably because in those days her family were not likely to view the courtship of her singing master with a favourable eye, Mrs. Radclyffe-Hall decided that it should be conducted abroad. I believe there was also some question of bringing a hesitating suitor to the point by an apparent flight. In any case, she decided to move to Belgium and she settled in Bruges, with a child who had already had double pneumonia once and who proceeded to have it again, besides being a martyr to bronchial asthma. I think there is little doubt that this enforced residence in the Low Countries was a factor in the development of the lung trouble which attacked her later, was never properly diagnosed or treated and which left her lungs in so ravaged a condition. Children and young people are marvellously uncomplaining. They accept philosophically such treatment as is meted out to them. But many years afterwards, when an X-ray of the lungs revealed the damage, and close questioning elicited memories of the asthma, of very exhausting coughing, or periods of general illness, of pneumonia, pleurisy and so forth, I remember Professor Lapiccirella of Florence saying to me: 'It is a mystery that she ever recovered and lived. By all ordinary reckoning she should have died. She must very often have felt terribly ill!'

The story of her mother's married life with Visetti is a trivial and a rather sordid one. After the marriage they settled down with Mrs. Visetti's mother in a large house in Earl's Court where Visetti pursued – very successfully – his profession as a singing-teacher; actually as professor of singing attached to the Royal College of Music, and he and his wife proceeded to spend on their own social aspirations and amenities the greater part of the income received from the Radclyffe-Hall trust for the maintenance and education of the child who was sole heir to the estate. 'Nottie', an amiable but I suspect very inexpensive governess, was succeeded by day schools in the neighbourhood, the best of which seems to have been one kept by a Miss Coles, which had numbered among its earlier pupils Edy Craig and the Vanbrugh sisters, Violet and Irene. A short period of attending King's College was followed by a year in Dresden at a pension where the girls were allowed one bath a week ... that completed John's 'education'....

Her home life was passed among the incessant and violent quarrelling of her mother and stepfather and her companions were his pupils who in some cases boarded in the house. Very early in life she herself showed remarkable musical capacity and a genuine talent for improvisation and composition, but entirely without the necessary elements of industry and perseverance. At some stage of her adolescence,

Nikisch, the great German conductor, was her stepfather's guest and listened to her performance on the piano. He was genuinely impressed by the originality of her talent and asked her to put everything else aside, come to Germany and study composition as his pupil. He also elicited that she could not read a note of music and did not know in what key she was playing . . . she utterly refused to contemplate a life of hard work and application and that was that. . . .

She had composed verses ever since her earliest childhood, and quite soon had begun to do so (as she invariably did in her maturer years) at the piano, fitting them to her own settings so that words and music came to birth simultaneously. The words were written down and many of them were subsequently published. The settings remained only in her memory, she being incapable of transcribing them, and were usually forgotten. I would sometimes get really angry with her when I found that some original and delightful little tune that had greatly pleased me had casually wandered out of her mind to the land of lost music.

Once I got hold of a young musician, an Indian, and got him to listen to her playing and to transcribe the settings chord by chord. One of them, 'The Last Cuckoo', was published by Chappel and Company, and sung by a number of well-known singers . . . but all this was of course merely the versatility that had been her father's undoing and against which he had warned her. Throughout her adolescence and her maturity until the age of thirty-four, she was idle, bone idle, spending her days, as soon as she became mistress of her own time, in pleasure; in hunting, travelling, writing an occasional poem, in entertaining and being entertained. And periodically, from the age of seventeen and onwards, falling in and out of love.

She was exceedingly handsome, had plenty of charm, plenty of intelligence, plenty of money, no education to speak of and was out exclusively to enjoy herself and to give others a good time. She systematically over-smoked, anything and everything, including green cigars. Drank freely on occasion but only in congenial company and never in her life felt the shadow of a craving for liquor (nicotine was her craving and in those days to crave was to have ...) and drove her cousin Jane Randolph (later Caruth) all over the States in a primitive car with one spark-plug at the back and a revolver handy for obstreperous negroes. There was also an aggressive bull-terrier, Charlie, as auxiliary protection.

I have in my possession a little leather-bound album with leaves of different colours: in it are written down, by her mother or grandmother, her earliest attempts at verse, beginning when she was three years old. So far as she or I could see when we examined them they show no talent or promise of any kind, no imagination or sense of rhythm: they are about flowers and 'birdies' and redolent of the atmosphere diffused by the simple old American dame, her grandmother, and by her entirely brainless mother. There is, however, one prophetic touch: one of the earliest is a love song, composed, I think, at the age of five. There are only four lines, of which the last is: 'No wonder the birdies love you, dear!'...

Of her earliest days, beyond the ill-treatment she suffered, I know very little. She hated dolls, loved drums and noisy toys, but such tastes are common to many girl children and might seem to have had little if any significance had the future not confirmed the fact of her sexual inversion. That her passionate temper was early developed is evidenced by her own memory of lying flat on her face in a new white plush coat in Kensington Gardens as a protest against being put back into her pram or mailcart when she desired to walk.

She was a beautiful child to look at. There is a life-size painting of her at five years old which her grandmother commissioned from Mrs. Katinka Amyat, the leading child portraitist of her day. It hung on the line at the Royal Academy and is the acme of photographic convention. A blue-eyed, golden haired little girl in a muslin frock and white socks sitting on a flowery bank, holding a bunch of oxeye daisies. But the child has beautiful features and looks out at you with brave honest eyes and an enchanting, jovial half-smile. . . .

There is a much earlier portrait. A photograph done in infancy of a sturdy-looking baby with silky fair down on its well-shaped head, propped upon a fur rug. Its fists are clenched and its expression fierce; there is a quite definite resemblance to the Radclyffe Hall of later years when she had made up her mind about anything and meant to see it through. . . . No one would doubt for a moment that this was a male child, and indeed, as I write this, a memory crops up that she was told at one time that throughout her infancy strangers always mistook her for a boy. She was still very young when she shed the baptismal name of Margaerite, selected by her mother, and became known to her friends as Peter . . . a name that later was replaced so universally by John that for years many people knew her by no other. It was on the title page of her first published novel that John Radclyffe-Hall became: 'Radclyffe Hall'.

Later photographs show her, as I said before, shy and unhappy-looking at about eleven years of age standing beside her stepfather; in her very early teens as a beautiful child with the melancholy eyes of her maturity, with a straight fringe and with unusually long and luxuriant fair hair. Later still comes a series, taken by society photographers during her adolescence, when her mother, refusing to be baffled by the aquiline nose and a severity of contour more suited to a youth than to a débutante, evolved the fiction that she resembled Gainsborough's female portraits and proceeded to impose her illusion by means of many ruffles, soft draperies and plumed hats. It was a period filled for John with embarrassment and helpless resentment, but it had to be endured until her twenty-first birthday brought her freedom . . . and the information that her mother, despite the sketchy education she had received, had managed to overspend the 'maintenance' allowance to the tune of £12,000. She told me that when she showed surprise and enquired how such a considerable debt had been incurred her mother flew into a violent rage and expressed deep endignation that a daughter should dare to question her parent's expenditure. But by that time the relations between them had long since been strained to breaking point; the situation being intensified by the mother's suspicions that her daughter was not what she considered 'normal'. This was, of course, only a suspicion, as she had absolutely no evidence to go on, but even the suspicion further inflamed her initial dislike and John told me of an occasion when her mother, in a blind fury, flew at her and tore her hat (and some of her hair with it) from her head. One of Visetti's most eminent pupils, who lived in the house as a member of the household, told me later that John's life at that time was sheer misery and that she had seen her mother 'go for her' and belabour her with her fists!

It was at this time also that John was called upon to protect her grandmother, when the old lady came to her in tears, having been struck by her daughter.

It is hardly surprising that as soon as she was free to do so and had control of her income, John left such a 'home' and took a house with her grandmother where the two of them could live in peace. That house was the corner one at the junction of Church Street, Kensington, and Campden House Terrace . . . I do not know how long they lived there but have an idea that although John, as time passed, travelled a lot and spent long periods in America, she returned to Campden House Terrace at intervals and that it remained her grandmother's home until her death. I know that at one time, after spending over a year in America touring the country, but living chiefly in Washington with her mother's relations, she became homesick (as she always did when she was long absent from England) and returned to London and to her grandmother bringing with her her widowed cousin, Jane Randolph, and the latter's three children, two boys and a girl. The children became exceedingly fond of John and the eldest boy, Decan (his brother did not survive childhood), came to visit us when we were together at Cadogan Court during the First World War.

Jane Randolph (by that time not only re-married to Harry Caruth, but widowed a second time) also visited us during the war when we had settled into our first unfurnished home, 'Chip Chase', Hadley Wood.

I think she was as great a surprise, and one might almost say as great a shock, to John as she was to me. John had described a plain young woman with projecting teeth but with a perfect figure, lovely hands and feet and masses of long and beautiful auburn hair. A woman always exquisitely dressed and of such charm that John, in her first youth, was the successful one of many adorers who flocked around her and strove for her favour. She and Jane had shared all kinds of youthful escapades in addition to their wanderings in the antediluvian car. There was the occasion when they left a Christmas feast of terrapin soup and champagne in such a condition that Jane greeted the frosty night with the remark: 'I want to schlide . . .', did so with catastrophic results and was helped home and upstairs past the bedroom door of a prim mother by John, who had only survived owing to a head of iron. . . . There was another story, very different, of her insisting upon accompanying John into hospital for the removal of an impacted wisdom tooth and occupying an emergency cot in her room with a devotion undeterred by the acute sickness that was always John's reaction to anaesthetics.

Anyway, the picture in my mind had been that of a hard-going, reckless and somewhat fickle but loyal-hearted seductress, who had managed to capture John's, at that time, rather volatile fancy and to hold it through various vicissitudes for several years. I awaited her arrival with a friendly interest and some curiosity. So, I am quite sure, did John, who was in any case determined to offer every hospitality that wartime conditions (it was in 1918) would allow. We found ourselves entertaining a stout, ageing American dame. (John had forgotten the detail that her attractive cousin had been many years her senior: when one is in one's twenties an additional ten or fifteen years only enhance attraction.) Our guest had heavy jowls and an elaborately piled coiffure of hair that was still abundant but had assumed that unpleasant brindle of auburn and grey that is almost mauve. She was smartly and tightly upholstered in expensive clothes and seemed very prosperous, but her expression reflected the discontent of her mind. Her conversation was a tissue of cranky, prim and hypercritical strictures upon the behaviour of her children, the upbringing of her grandchildren and life in general . . . but only one sentence remained permanently in John's memory and mine. Offering her a cup of tea on her arrival at our war-rationed abode, John enquired: 'Do you have milk in your tea now, Jane?' and Jane replied firmly: 'Cream, please. . . .' As neither of us had seen cream for four years the request made an indelible impression.

The visit, despite all our efforts, was not a success. She no longer really liked John, who was quite unable to like her, and she definitely disliked me and, incredible as it seemed after so many years, resented my existence. . . . When she left us she returned to America and we never saw her again, though her daughter came over and did visit us with a nebulous husband and a thoroughly tiresome little girl named Jane after her grandmother, by whom, I believe, she was afterwards adopted. Sometimes in later years we used to smile, John and I, over the 'cream, please' incident and other details that I have now forgotten.

Occasionally letters came from Decan and from the daughter, Winefred (full of complaints, hers were, of her mother's attempted interferences and difficult ways), but somehow I don't think John ever really linked up the unpleasing guest of 1918 with the boon companion of her salad days or even with the cousin who had lived with her and her grandmother for a time at Campden House Terrace and who was the mother of two unruly boys and a girl.

It never seems to have struck John that she took over a heavy burden in assuming complete financial responsibility for an impecunious young widow and three children and carting them over from the States; a responsibility that only ended at Jane's re-marriage, again to a Southerner, but this time to a very rich man. In all the years I lived with her I never knew John to be turned from any purpose by difficulties or deterred by potential responsibility, and I think

24

the story of her friendship with Jane Randolph-Caruth shows that this was an early and fundamental characteristic. I may add that, responsibility once assumed, it was never in any circumstances repudiated; I am convinced that there does not live, and never has lived, anyone who can truthfully say that Radclyffe Hall failed them, or ever let them down.

Of course there are many dropped stitches in the fabric of my knowledge of her early life: so many things she had forgotten herself or did not think worth telling. So many things, alas, that she did tell me and that I have forgotten.

Her first serious falling in love, at the age of seventeen or eighteen, was, she always told me, with a voice . . . The lovely pure soprano voice of her stepfather's pupil, Agnes Nicols. . . . For several years she worshipped and served and followed that voice to and fro on the initial stages of a big career. Wherever engagements in opera, concert or oratorio took the young singer, there also went John, listening, encouraging, sympathizing and adoring. Holding cloaks, mufflers, bouquets, gargles and inhalers; in hotels, lodgings, trains and dressing-rooms, her existence entirely regulated by the imperious demands of that wonderful voice. . . . I can remember it myself, as I first heard it, at Covent Garden, after looking superciliously at the then almost unknown English name on the programme. It was unique, and once heard quite unforgettable: a strange blend of woman, choir-boy and angel, and, in justice to Alberto Visetti it must be admitted, most beautifully produced. . . . I cannot wonder that John, adolescent, intensely musical and emotional, listening day by day in her own home to the gradual evolution of this exquisite thing, fell deeply in love both with the voice and the singer. Agnes Nichols was seven years her senior, an earnest student and steadily determined to succeed. Love, if it came, must be harnessed to that ambition,

25

which, as we now know, was to be fully realized, she passed on her triumphant way none the less surely because John, whom the Lord had not designed to be a satellite, grew weary after a time of dressing rooms and theatrical paraphernalia and glamour; of the despair that attended a trifling hoarseness, of all life subordinated to that supertyrant, a singer's voice, and at some unspecified date departed to fresh woods and pastures new on a visit to her mother's relations in America. . . .

I know that Agnes Nichols has always remembered John with affection, is a great admirer of her work, and, but for the fact that she was ill at the time, would have sung the solo at her Requiem Mass.

There was another American cousin of whom she became fond, or who at any rate attracted her for a time and in John's case, though she was by no means always emotionally attracted to those of whom she became fond, she inevitably developed a measure of affection for and a protective sense towards those with whom she fell in love. . . . The latter impulse might spring up in her instantaneously and fully armed, irrespective of the merits of its object, but invariably that other side of her curiously complex make-up: that generous, highly spiritual element that in the end burnt up any lesser thing and pervaded and possessed her entirely, would hasten to discover and, failing that, to manufacture in the object of her attraction qualities that justified affection or admitted of sheltering care. . . .

Such a process, I think, must have taken place long before I knew her, in the circumstances of her connection with the young cousin Dorothy Diehl (the only daughter of her mother's brother) whom she met for the first time in America and who returned with her to England and afterwards travelled with her for a time in Europe.

She seems to have made a habit of bringing home American cousins! In this case, Dorothy Diehl was younger than herself, which facilitated the protective attitude. She was plump and very pretty in a blue-eyed, golden-haired, pink and white style suggestive of the Dutch maiden of the musical comedies of our youth. She certainly had a charming mouth with deeply indented upturned corners and an infectious smile, and when I met her long afterwards I thought her very amusing; but her wit had a cutting edge to it and her nature a crudity that was revealed in the coarsest hands I ever remember seeing on any woman. At the time I came to know her she had an immensely fat baby and had been married for a number of years to the composer Robert Coningsby Clarke. She had fallen violently in love with him while still making her home with John and as they were both young and he relatively impecunious (his subsequently successful career as a ballad writer not having yet materialized), John had helped the course of what she was assured was true love to run more smoothly by supplying an allowance which was continued for many years. . . . It lasted longer, I think, than the true love, but was finally discontinued when Dorothy Clarke, despite repeated warnings from John, persisted in making mischief between her and an old friend.

Dorothy Clarke is dead now, and you might well say, '*de mortuis*', but this record is to be the truth, the whole truth and nothing but the truth and the truth in this case is that in an affair that was doubtless lightly undertaken on both sides John ended by giving a good deal, both morally and financially, and received in return not even elementary gratitude or loyalty.

And, you may begin to ask, where in all this do we find any traces of Radclyffe Hall, the future writer?

All through the years whose vicissitudes I have tried to indicate she was, as I said before, resolutely and remorselessly idle and bent exclusively on making of life a pleasant pastime.

Such energy as she possessed (and in spite of a far from robust constitution, her nervous system was as young and as reckless as she was herself. It supplied all the necessary fuel and she was often very energetic indeed), was devoted to love-making, to hunting (sometimes five days a week), to riding and mastering unmanageable horses; to rushing about by car, boat or train (at that time the air was not available!) to any new place that took her fancy; to all and anything but mental effort, which was represented in her programme by occasional verses that arose spontaneously and unsought into her consciousness, were written down and received, it must be admitted, even in those days a measure of careful polishing and revision.

They were published, those verses, and, to give the first date I have mentioned (and I mention it for a very good reason to which I shall return later), before 1908 three volumes of those verses had appeared and had met with considerable success. The first volume was produced by John and Edward Bumpus, the publication being paid for by her proud grandmother! The subsequent volumes were published by Chapman and Hall. I have pored over them many times, and so has their author, and neither of us was able to find anything worthy of survival in the first two volumes; in fact long before her death she made a determined effort to destroy any existing copies of the volumes in question, hoping to consign them to total oblivion. (One of the results of her efforts has been that collectors of her work are ready nowadays to pay quite a high price for either of those despised offspring of her idle youth!) Nevertheless, at the time of publication, these lyrics met with a very good reception indeed and were very favourably criticized by the *Athenaeum* and other serious journals. . . . John never got over her astonishment at the fact: she was thoroughly ashamed of her Juvenilia. But the verses, and the volumes that followed them (one of them with an appreciation by Robert Cunninghame Graham) also met with another kind of success. Perhaps partly because, as I said earlier, they had usually been written at the piano, they were eagerly seized upon by a number of well-known song writers of the time and many of them were set to music by Liza Lehmann, Coleridge Taylor, Teresa Del Riego, Easthope Martin, Mrs. George Batten and others and were sung at the ballad concerts that were the predecessors of the B.B.C. and by all those enthusiastic amateurs who performed in the home! Most of these songs are seldom heard nowadays, but one has survived one war and is working its way steadily through another: Robert Coningsby Clarke's setting of her lyric 'The Blind Ploughman' (a poor and over-theatrical setting in my opinion) . . . the plain words of a puritan peasant set to an emotional organ obligato. But Dame Clara Butt, Chaliapin, Powell Edwards, Paul Robeson, and, much later, Rossi-Lemeni, to mention only five singers, have used that song as a powerful appeal for those who had lost their sight in war, and not long ago I turned on my radio and suddenly heard the strains of 'The Blind Ploughman'.

Too much dwelling, you may say, upon a few volumes of inferior verse; but the fact is that much of the verse in her third, fourth and fifth volumes was far from inferior and the quality of such lyrics as 'The Blind Ploughman' was the first serious indication of things to come.

John's deliberate mental indolence, her absorption in sport, her restlessness, her carefree, careless youth were to meet their Waterloo at Homburg, where she went for some frivolous purpose in 1907 and there met my cousin Mabel Veronica Batten, Mrs. George Batten, who was to alter her entire outlook on life and the whole course of her existence.

When John, at the age of twenty-seven, first saw her and fell head and heart and soul in love with her, 'Ladye', as she was called by all her intimate friends, was still, at fifty, a very lovely woman. She was no longer physically, perhaps, what she had been when Baron de Meyer took the photograph of her that has so often been reproduced, but she had always been infinitely more attractive than her more classically 'beautiful' sister (Mrs. Eddie Bourke, afterwards Lady Clarendon) and she kept the charm of her perfectly set eyes, chiselled and slightly tiptilted nose and of one of the loveliest mouths I ever saw, until her death eight years later. If she was no longer slim, she was no more than graciously ample and she had great dignity and length of line. She had that characteristically Irish colouring of a pale complexion, dark blue eyes and dark hair and not only her beautifully produced singing voice, but also her speaking voice, were quite enchanting. All of this John saw and heard and loved, but she very soon realized that Ladye was not merely a lovely woman; she was also exceedingly intelligent, cultured in the extreme and a personality in every sense of the word. She accepted homage as a matter of course; she had always received it. She reciprocated affection in full measure but she had no intention of sharing her life to any extent with what she regarded as a half-educated young cub who ignored all the important aspects of a civilized existence and preferred hunting to literature, music or the arts. . . . She herself was acknowledged in London as a patroness of music; she was one of those who sponsored the young Mischa Elman and the newly arrived Percy

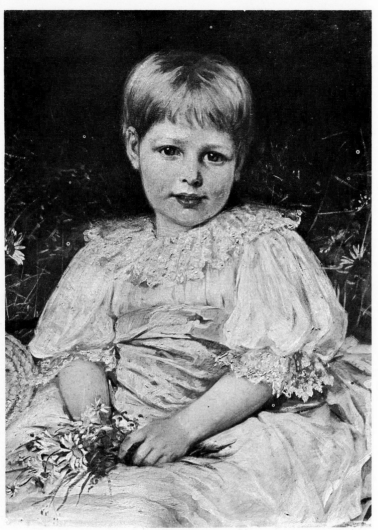

Radclyffe Hall at the age of five. Oil painting by Katinka Amyat.

Radclyffe Hall soon after she met Una Troubridge. Oil painting
by Charles Buchel.

Grainger. Her own voice was a mezzo-soprano, not powerful, but it was most perfectly trained and she, Mme. Felix Zemon and Mrs. Henschel were the leading 'amateur' lieder singers of their day. She always accompanied herself and was a composer of some talent. She spoke French quite as well as her own language, and had some knowledge of Italian. She read voraciously everything that seemed to her worth while in the first two languages. . . . She was, as a matter of fact, physically indolent, but she very soon met John's adoring gaze with the brisk remark that people who had loved and been loved by her had always done something, been someone or in any case had used their brains. And so, in her immense desire to make herself worthy of someone she loved, John's real education began.

And not very long after she first met Ladye, John had a very severe accident which greatly facilitated these cultural aspirations. At that time, in addition to a flat in Tite Street, Chelsea, close to Ladye's house in Ralston Street, Tedworth Square, she had taken a lease of Highfield House, a large house in Malvern Wells in a situation that enabled her to hunt with three packs.

I never saw this house, but John told me it was modern, not particularly attractive, and that she took it because of its fine and spacious stables. She kept at least five horses at that time and their comfort was more important to her than her own. To the day of her death she hated to see a horse in a stall and I suspect an adequate supply of loose boxes to have been one of the factors in her taking Highfield.

Of the horses she owned, I do not know very much. But I know she took a great pride in the upkeep of her stables. There was a very handsome cob, Grey Dawn, which she sometimes brought to London and rode in the Row. There was a beloved and very wise hunter, Joseph, who was also

31

sometimes brought to London. I have photographs of Joseph and I have his hooves, mounted by Rowland Ward, in my possession. On one occasion during a run, Joseph was terribly cut with barbed wire, but the valiant horse ignored the injury and went on and it was not until the end of the run that the condition of his knees was discovered. The vet's only prescription, after the distracted John had led him home step by step, yard by yard, was a bullet. But John loved him dearly and he loved her, affection prevailed and saved his life; he was put in slings and was so amenable to her ministrations that he recovered and lived until old age brought infirmity and, like Raftery in the *Well of Loneliness*, of whom he was to some extent the prototype, he was shot in her presence.

But not all her horses were like Joseph. There was also Xenophon – a magnificent jumper with such a temper that her grooms refused to ride him and friends prophesied that he would kill her, which in the upshot he very nearly succeeded in doing. . . .

One day out hunting, an unmannerly amateur pounded them at a fence, Xenophon lost his temper in mid-air and came crashing down in the ditch, pitching his rider into it on her head while the interloper jumped over them both and missed her by inches. Farmers came to the rescue, Xenophon was none the worse and John, keen as mustard, decided that she was quite able to go on with the hunt which she proceeded to do, eventually riding ten miles home and only when she got there collapsing with severe concussion and a spinal injury.

She was very ill indeed; in fact at one time, as she used to relate with much amusement, an X-ray was taken of her neck and the doctor informed her it was suspected that she was a most interesting case in that she was alive and walking about with a broken neck. I remember her telling me that the doctor was so excited that he inquired there and then whether, in the event of a second X-ray confirming these suspicions, she would be willing to attend at the hospitals as an exhibit! The second X-ray, however, to his unconcealed disappointment, proved that the neck was intact. But she was nonetheless suffering severely from shock and the aftermath of concussion, had much spinal pain and terrible headaches, I believe, and since she was an excellent sailor and, like her father, adored the sea, it was suggested that a sea voyage would accelerate recovery.

As Ladye also adored the sea and was an even better sailor than John there was no reluctance in following the doctor's advice and before very long they had left England together, bound for the Canary Islands.

And here it may be noted that to all intents and purposes this incident marked the decline of John's sporting activities. She did not at once stop hunting, which in those days she dearly loved, she kept her horses and rode when in London, but nevertheless, the end of that phase was in sight. Hunting meant English country life throughout the winter months, she and Ladye had by then definitely made common cause, and while an English winter might be very agreeable to hearty folk who shot and hunted, Ladye had less than no use for England except during the summer and she was increasingly conscious of the charms of Morocco, the Canary Islands, Corsica, Alassio, Rome and even, when it came to that, of Monte Carlo!

She knew nothing of horses and was afraid of them. Her fear was not diminished by the fact that Xenophon, when she was introduced to him in his palatial loose box, scented her timidity and ran at her with his teeth bared!

As for riding herself, a habit was duly ordered and a quiet

mount carefully prepared, but after one attempt John warmly agreed with her that horsemanship was not her bent. There was a story that she would tell against herself. When as a young woman she had been in India, her husband, who was secretary to the Viceroy, had decided to teach her to ride. Having very quickly realized that she had not been born with good hands, he had exclaimed: 'Feel his mouth, Mabel, you must feel his mouth' . . . and she, leaning as far forward as she dared, had replied: 'I can't, George; I can't reach it!'

To all this must be added the very understandable fact that, after John's accident, Ladye was always nervous and uneasy when she was hunting and must have made her anxiety deliberately apparent. In any case, it was quite obvious that two completely divergent ways of life could not be combined and that Ladye's views would naturally prevail. It was also obvious that, particularly after their voyage to Orotava, in John herself brawn was giving way to brain and she was eager for more voyages and exploration of pastures new.

By the time I came to know her, in 1915, hunting was a distant memory and she had not been on a horse for several years. She never again hunted (by that time she had acquired a horror of killing) and she did not ride again until she and I went to Lynton together for brief holidays, during what was then known as the Great War, and spent most of our time astride a couple of local ponies.

However, in spite of the humanitarian scruples that now forbade hunting, or any blood sports, her eye would always kindle if she happened to meet hounds and she would say to me: 'Aren't I unregenerate! I'd love to follow; there's something in hunting that you never find in anything else. . . .' She would talk of setting out in the early mornings through a countryside that was not yet awake, and then add hastily: 'Yes, but that was cubbing, the most brutal thing of all. . . .' And even in her most unregenerate days, stag hunting had always aroused her horror and indignation.

And so, gradually and with the passing of hunting and of Joseph, Highfield went, the horses went, and life assumed the pattern that suited Ladye, and by that time suited John very well also.

Early in their friendship, George Batten, who was about twenty-five years older than his wife and had for years filled the functions of a devoted and indulgent father, slipped out of life, relieved to know that she would still have love and protection. He had grown very fond of Johnnie, as he called her, demanded her constant presence in his last illness and knew that he could trust her.

The house in Ralston Street was given up, as was the flat in Tite Street, and they took a flat at 59 Cadogan Square and bought the White Cottage, Malvern Wells. In those days John was a rich woman, Ladye was quite well provided for and money being plentiful these two homes could not only be easily maintained, but they could be easily left in reliable hands when their owners wished to go further afield. In some five or six years they wandered a good deal. To Morocco; a second time (I think) to the Canary Islands. They spent one summer, and I believe also one winter, at Alassio where they took a furnished villa, and one winter and spring in Rome, where John acquired Roman fever and very nearly came to an abrupt end. The aftermath of the emanations from the then undrained Pontine Marshes never really died out of her system and would crop up at all sorts of unexpected moments. Rome they loved; not classical Rome, but the Rome of their faith, for Ladye had been a Catholic since early youth and John had been received into the Church not long after they became friends. In Rome, therefore, they attended many religious functions, under the guidance of Cardinal Gasquet, who also obtained for them a private audience with His Holiness Pius X. The saintly peasant-Pope abhorred ceremony and his humility deprecated homage. John has told me of how the Cardinal warned them to omit the customary three genuflexions and of how, when in her shyness and reverence she forgot and fell on to her knees, the Cardinal clutched her by the scruff of the neck and hauled her to her feet, hissing 'Get up! What did I tell you!'

In any case it was Ladye who was the success of that audience. Her Italian was quite tolerable, while John's had not yet come into existence. Ladye was self-possessed and said and did the right thing, putting the Pope (who was himself a desperately shy man) at his ease, while John hovered in the background tongue-tied. The result was that when the Cardinal presented two photographs for signature, Ladye's bore a lengthy inscription: '*Alla diletta figlia Veronica . . .*' while John's received only an unadorned autograph, to which the kindly Cardinal, fearing that she might be disappointed, added the date and the fact that it had been signed at a private audience. . . . And now Pius X is long dead, and has already been beatified. Cardinal Gasquet and Mabel Veronica Batten have been followed by Radclyffe Hall . . . I wonder if they have all met and discussed that audience and laughed over the incident of the photographs?

But life was not only Rome and Papal audiences and religious ceremonies: there was also Monte Carlo and the tables, for though Ladye might be both pious and cultured she was no prig. In fact, inveterate gambler as John might easily have become, it was Ladye who at a certain time of year was wont to develop what John called the Riviera wheeze and the Monte Carlo cough, hinting at the desirability of avoiding the English winter and seeking refuge in a warmer climate. John used to say that it was surprising that wherever they planned to go for a holiday the route as worked out by Ladye invariably found its way through Monte Carlo.

But when they got there Ladye was very moderate in her playing. She liked to potter along in a quiet way, getting tremendous excitement out of small losses or gains. Not so John; when she played at all, she went the pace and went it hard, and on one occasion, fully recognizing her own inability to pull up, she marched in upon the bank manager at Monte Carlo, and, having cashed a cheque that would cover hotel expenses and the journey home, requested him to cancel the balance of her letter of credit.

I like to dwell upon those years. They were amongst the happiest of her life, for they were shared with a most delightful, sympathetic and versatile companion. I, who had known Ladye since my childhood and grew to know her very well before her death, can vouch for that. And if those years were apparently idle and pleasure-seeking, they nonetheless saw the gradual development of John's true personality. For whether they travelled or stayed in England, whether they rusticated at the White Cottage in Malvern Wells or led a social life in London: opera – theatres – concerts – receptions and the reciprocal entertaining in private houses and flats that had not yet been superseded by the restaurant and the night club, always they read and read and read, in English, in French, even occasionally, to judge by a few volumes in Ladye's library, in Italian. Ladye would read aloud to John, as I also did later through so many years, and books and their writers, music and its composers or exponents, the theatre, the Russian opera and ballet when they came, were all woven into the texture of their daily life which was lived to a great extent among people with exceptional brains, people who 'did things' and who counted for something in the world. Through those years John's devotion burned with a steady light and was returned; her fancy did stray once, it is true, but it was a trivial, passing lapse, broke no bones and left no aftermath. It is hardly worth recording, Ladye dismissed the incident with a tolerant smile, and no one but John, scourging herself for infidelity, gave it any great importance.

At intervals during those years, poems were written and more carefully polished and revised. Three volumes were published: *Songs of Three Counties* in 1907, I think, *Poems of the Past and Present* in 1910 or 1911, and in 1914, *The Forgotten Island*.

The contents are of unequal quality, but there is plenty of good verse in them and some that is eminently worthy of survival. She herself revised them not long ago, 'beheading' a number of the lyrics and setting the stamp of her more mature approval upon others.

But what is more important to my mind is that it was during those years when she was already over thirty, in the intervals of writing verse, that she began to try her hand at prose and wrote some half dozen short stories. I have got the manuscripts of all these early efforts, written and re-written, scored out and corrected; they bear, in this respect, a great resemblance to those of later years. Whatever the intrinsic merit of the stories, one thing emerges clearly. The future talent was stirring in her, something was asking insistently to be born, something in her nature was not easily satisfied with what she produced and reluctantly, intermittently, inexpertly, she was awakening to self-criticism, she was beginning to try to work. . . .

These tentative efforts at prose were undoubtedly met by Ladye with sympathy and encouragement; as evidence of the fact I could produce a number of exercise books in which (neither of them possessing or knowing how to use a typewriter, nor apparently thinking of employing a typist) she has laboriously made in her clearest handwriting a fair copy of the defaced and almost illegible manuscripts.

Whether she would have liked the life that (proudly and joyfully!) was mine for so many years; a life of watching, serving and subordinating everything in existence to the requirements of an overwhelming literary inspiration and industry, guarding and sustaining a physique that was never equal to John's relentless perseverance or to the strain she compelled it to bear, is a question that Ladye was never asked to answer. But one thing is certain. She was delighted that John had a brain to use and that she should try to use it. She had sufficient taste and judgment to recognize talent, even in the egg, and having done so, she took steps that led, indirectly and long after her death, to the writing of *The Unlit Lamp* and of all its successors.

Being convinced that John's short stories showed signs of genuine talent she began to wish for their publication and the only means that occurred to her of forwarding this aim was to show them to a potential publisher. She therefore sent them, with an explanatory letter, to an acquaintance who was none other than William Heinemann, at that time at the height of his fame as the discoverer and publisher of unsuspected talent. This was, I think, in 1913.

The results exceeded everyone's most sanguine expectations. She very promptly received a letter from him informing her that the manuscripts she had sent him were of such a quality that he wished to meet the author, and he suggested that they should both lunch with him and talk things over. I wish I had that letter now. I am pretty sure that either Ladye or John must have treasured it, as they were both of them immensely impressed by the result of Ladye's venture. But it must at some time have been mislaid or destroyed. Or for that matter it may still be lurking among John's multitudinous papers; in any case I have never come across it.

The invitation, however, was accepted and the luncheon took place; an exceedingly proud and delighted Ladye escorting an exceedingly shy and embarrassed John, who, to her utter amazement, was informed by Mr. Heinemann that not only did her stories show signs of real talent but that one of them, in his opinion, was among the best short stories that had ever come his way. I am not sure that he did not say, in his genuine excitement at having, as he believed, discovered a fine writer, that it was *the* best short story ever submitted for his approval.

The story in question was *The Career of Mark Anthony Brakes* and it has never been published. Circumstances, as I shall explain, delayed its publication, and when, many years later, John might have included it in her first and only volume of short stories, she decided that whatever might be its merits of style and construction, what had, when she wrote it, been the originality of its theme: the sudden and disastrous breakdown of civilization and self-control in an educated negro under the stress of sexual emotion, had since then been treated and exhausted by other writers, both white and coloured, and that her story had definitely missed the boat.

To return to the fateful luncheon, however. Mr. Heinemann repeated and indeed elaborated his favourable criticism of the stories, and even John's natural shyness, melted by this meed of praise, gave way and she said bluntly and hopefully: 'Then you are going to publish my stories, Mr. Heinemann?' To which he replied trenchantly: 'I will certainly do nothing of the kind. I am not going to present you to the public as the writer of a few short stories, however good they may be, and what is more, I do not want you to offer them to any periodical. You will set to work at once and write me a novel, and when it is finished I will publish it. . . .'

John was disappointed, disconcerted and moreover, as she told me more than once, positively appalled at the suggestion. She protested that she had not the faintest idea even of how to set about writing a novel, had never thought of undertaking a work of any length and felt quite certain that she would never be able to do it, would, as she put it, 'never stay the course'. 'Oh yes, you will', replied Mr. Heinemann. 'You don't know it yourself yet, but I know it. You can and you will and you will bring it to me.'

She never saw him again. She was not at that time ready to modify her entire way of life and make the sacrifice demanded by so great an effort and a programme of work on a large scale, nor, I think, did Ladye urge it. She herself had no real conception of the powers latent in her friend, no idea that any sacrifices of leisure and pleasure would bear fruit in the production of such literature as she would have been the first to appreciate. Their mode of life was, in every way, fulfilling to them both and it never occurred to them to alter it. Mr. Heinemann's appreciation had been a pleasant incident and a gratification and it was disappointing that he had not been prepared to add a volume of short stories under a fine imprint to the five existing volumes of verse. But it certainly never entered either of their heads that his unerring perspicacity had again spotted a winner and that a distant future was to justify every word that he spoke.

Nor, looking back with the eye of one who knows the sequel, can I regret the fact that John was not, at that time, able to decipher the writing on the wall. True, she was by then a very different person from the embryonic youngster who had met Ladye at Homburg. Athletic diversions had receded into the background and she had to a great extent come into her destined inheritance of intellectual, artistic and religious understanding. But her experiences had been chiefly pleasurable and, while a reciprocated devotion to an eminently worthy object had done much to develop in her the latent unselfishness and tenderness that had hitherto lacked scope, she had, apart from the unhappiness of her childhood, and passing storms of emotional despair, never suffered deeply, as she was to do during the years that elapsed before she began to fulfil Mr. Heinemann's prophecy.

All the same, even if they were unproductive of intellectual fruit, I like to think of those years from 1907 until 1913 . . . Except for one passing emotional storm to which I have already alluded, they were so happy; the happiest she had ever known, or was perhaps ever to know. An easy, congenial, interesting existence in perfect company, with her newly-awakened perceptions rising one by one into her consciousness and welcomed and fostered with sympathy and understanding. . . . No; in justice to myself, I will not, cannot, say that she was not to know an equal happiness later, and many times in our long pilgrimage together. Perhaps she was to rise to greater heights of true happiness such as are only reached by those who have plumbed the depths of sorrow and suffering. But all the same, there was an idyllic, peaceful happiness in those years that was all their own, and how glad I am to think that she had them.

I have said that circumstances as well as inclination interfered with her attempting to obey Mr. Heinemann's behest. She and Ladye might well cling closely to their pleasant mode of life; they were not to enjoy it much longer.

During the early summer of that same year as their car (a heavy limousine) was passing the crossroads at Burford on the way to the White Cottage at Malvern Wells, it was literally charged from the near side by a small open car driven by a lady who met the emergency by mistaking the accelerator for the brake. The violence of the first impact was such that it flung the heavy car over against a stone wall which it demolished, while the aggressor proceeded to pound it repeatedly before her engine stalled. The big car ended up on its side, terribly shattered (the body-makers subsequently expressed surprise that anyone had come out of it alive), the maid who was sitting in front beside the chauffeur was injured, John was practically unhurt but Ladye lay unconscious in the bottom of the car with several broken ribs, an injury to a vertebra of her neck and bleeding from severe cuts on her head. The chauffeur, who had not been hurt, lost his head and wept hysterically, but fortunately there were people about who helped John to extricate Ladye and who carried her into a house near by. Her injuries were skilfully attended to and she had every possible care and treatment but it was many weeks before they were able to proceed on their journey to the White Cottage. She was an invalid for as many months; she never, I think, completely recovered, and moreover, when she died of a stroke less than two years later, the doctors were of opinion that she had suffered the first seizure at the time of the accident.

They did not go abroad again but spent that summer and the next at the White Cottage, which they had bought together and which she dearly loved. They were there in August 1914 when the war came and they returned to London and that was almost the last that Ladye saw of the cottage. It had to be sold early in 1916 when prices were rising and incomes were diminishing and when it was also decided to move from Cadogan Square to a less expensive flat.

But meanwhile I had come into the picture and, little as any of us suspected it at the time, I had come to stay.

And here I am going to meet with a difficulty because, up to this period of John's life, I have been dealing exclusively with matters concerning her and other people, and of which she or others have told me. But as from August 1st, 1915, the story becomes also my own story, and it will be less easy to be completely objective. Moreover, since from the day of our meeting we were at first much together, and soon afterwards scarcely ever apart, it becomes difficult, or I am afraid it may be far from easy, to continue making this as I wish it to be, the story of Radclyffe Hall and not of Una Troubridge. . . .

To some extent I must inevitably enter in and I shall in any case try to be as critical of myself as I am of other people, but I shall also try to omit, so far as possible, my personal concerns and history.

However, it seems inevitable that I should describe our first meeting, or what was in point of fact our second meeting, but the first time that we realized one another's existence. I had once before met her, with Ladye, several years earlier at an afternoon reception in one of the old houses in

Cheyne Walk. Of that meeting small details remain in my mind to this day. The three of us sat and talked in the garden. Ladye, of course, I had always known and she introduced her friend. Of John I remember nothing at all. Of Ladye a rather adhesive tailor-made suit of the prevailing cut, made of a grey material with a white stripe that dazzled and made one blink, and what we should now consider an overwhelming hat. They drove me home to St. George's Square, where I was then living, but the meeting had no sequel; nothing warned us of what the future held in store.

In 1915 I was living in a tiny house in Bryanston Street; for very good reasons I was deeply depressed and intensely lonely. But for these facts I might not have accepted an invitation from my cousin Lady Clarendon to have tea with her in Cambridge Square on August 1st . . . she added that 'Mabel' would also be coming. I did not like Lady Clarendon. She was an ex-beauty, always jealous of her more attractive sister and, having married Lord Clarendon as her second husband, she had become, as Violet, Duchess of Rutland, expressed it to Ladye, 'very Countessy'. But I had always liked Ladye and admired her, and, as I have said, I was lonely and so I accepted. . . .

Of Ladye on that second occasion I have no recollection, but I can still see John as I saw her on that day, as clearly as if she stood before me now. She was then thirty-four years of age and very good indeed to look upon. At that time, short hair in a woman was almost unknown and she had not yet cut hers. Ladye would have been horrified at the mere suggestion! It was silver-blonde, and she ruthlessly disposed of its great length and abundance (it reached nearly to her knees and its growth defied frequent pruning) by wearing it in tight plaits closely twisted round her small and admirably shaped head. Her complexion was clear and

45

pale, her eyebrows and very long lashes nearly as golden as her hair and her eyes a clear grey blue, beautifully set and with a curiously fierce, noble expression that reminded me of certain caged eagles at the Zoological Gardens! Her mouth was sensitive and not small. It could look very determined; indeed in those days it sometimes looked hard, but was liable to break into the most infectious, engaging and rather raffish smile that would spread to her eyes and banish the caged eagle. Her face and the line of her jaw were an unusually pure oval. From great-grandfather John Hall she had inherited an aquiline nose with delicate, tempered wings to the nostrils. From the mythical American-Indian, unusually high cheekbones. In any case it was not the countenance of a young woman but of a very handsome young man. Like her father she was only of medium height but so well-proportioned that she looked taller than she was and the very simple tailor-made clothes which she wore, even in those days, fostered the illusion. Her hands, and here again, they were not feminine hands, were quite beautiful and so were her feet. Altogether her appearance was calculated to arouse interest. It immediately aroused mine and for reasons much less obvious that interest was returned. Our friendship, which was to last through life and after it, dated from that meeting.

But there seemed to be many factors against it at the time. Kindly as she was towards me, Ladye most certainly felt no overwhelming desire for my incorporation in their daily life and John, I know, honestly believed that her feeling for me was just such another sudden fancy as she had experienced before. She was nothing if she was not honest and I remember her saying to me: 'How do I know if I shall care for you in six months time?...' As for me, I thought little and felt a great deal. I was swept along on a spate of feeling, of learning the endless aspects of this strange personality, and all I knew or cared about was that I could not, once having come to know her, imagine life without her. I had, at twenty-eight, as much consideration for Ladye or for anyone else as a child of six.

Being now nearly sixty, most of my vision works backwards and I can visualize what seemed at the time a mere vortex of impulses and coincidence and tragedy as a pattern that in retrospect seems to have had its definite purposes. But when the three of us were beset by conflicting emotions and loyalties we could not know that Ladye's death was imminent. We could not know that John was shortly to be left alone, and that the fact that her death brought John not only intense sorrow but also a measure of remorse (for, though her devotion to Ladye had never wavered, she blamed herself bitterly afterwards for having harboured another affection) would lead to her taking up an investigation that involved endless labour, patience and precision and developed in her that industry and perseverance in which she had always been so conspicuously lacking. We could not know that in that investigation I was to make the more important moves, was to work with her as her lieutenant in closest co-operation and was, for my part, to develop the qualities that would enable me to give her the service she would require when she settled down to her real purpose in life.

In 1915, all this was hidden in the impenetrable future. Ladye was merely not in robust health; her heart was supposed to need care and John was vigilant in sparing her any exertion. . . .

Of the doctors who had attended her, not one had suggested that dieting might be advisable for a blood pressure of well over 200 and of this potential peril we were blissfully unaware. She felt fairly well, and led her normal life with John, a life of which, during that summer, autumn and the succeeding months, I also became a part. I had my own flat and they were living at first in Cadogan Square and later, having sold the White Cottage and disposed of their flat, in a suite of rooms at the Vernon Court Hotel in Buckingham Palace Road, debating where they should pitch their tent. During the summer they came down to visit me in Brighton where I had taken my child and her nurse, and later we all went together to Watergate Bay in Cornwall. There my intimacy with John developed in the course of long walks and talks and drives in the local jingles. There I saw her for the first time in rough country clothes; heavy short-skirted tweeds unusual in those days, collars and ties and, I remember, a queer little green Heath hat with a pot-shaped crown. I also heard Ladye lament her complete absence of vanity and her indifference to the unbecoming effects of wind and rain . . . and day by day I fell more completely under the spell of her enthralling personality. She was so intensely alive, she could be so kind and so tender, and she was also so wilful, so humorous and, in those days, so intolerant! Her temper was so violent, so quickly spent, and her penitence, if she thought she had given pain, so extreme. . . . She was so intuitive, so intelligent and yet so naïve and simple. She was still a mass of sharp corners, prejudices and preconceptions that she was sure nothing was ever going to modify! She was at that time not only devout but, to my mind, bigoted in the extreme, and young as I was, and also devout, I rebelled at her militant theories. I remember saying to her: 'I believe you would be prepared to torture heretics . . . in another age you would have been a Torquemada . . .' and to this extent I was right: I had met for the first time in my life a born fanatic. Not, however, as I then suggested, one who would persecute others, but one who, if the need arose, would go to the pillory or the stake for her convictions, one who would go through fire and water, would never accept defeat and would fight the good fight through mental and physical suffering until, when the tormented body failed, the spirit blazed forth, brave, patient, and unafraid, and she rendered up her splendid soul to God.

But in the days of Watergate Bay if battle and martyrdom and many aspects of her complex nature lay hidden in the future, there were many characteristics that were obvious and that she had shown since childhood and one of these was her passionate devotion to animals, her indignant championship of them in suffering or neglect. This was a fundamental instinct that was later to appear in almost everything she wrote. Horses, as I have said, she loved and understood, though she had not then, as she did later, learned to love also the fox. Dogs large and small (she had no patience at all with the professed dog-lover who made size a qualification) she was never without. When I met her at Lady Clarendon's she was accompanied by a toy fox-terrier named Jill, a recent acquisition – an uninteresting and generally unsatisfactory little beast which, to my relief, was soon planted in a good home. But others remained and were frequently reinforced. There was Rufus, ageing at that time but deeply loved, and deeply mourned when he died. He was a big sable Welsh collie rescued from the Battersea Dogs' Home. She would say in later years that she sometimes heard him breathing at night in her bedroom and as she lay in bed a few days before she died she said to me quietly: 'Rufus is standing beside me with his head on my arm.' Fortune, a French bull bitch, was acquired soon after we met, the first in my time of an endless series, ranging

49

from a Great Dane weighing some five stone to a Yorkshire terrier who turned the scales at one pound and three quarters and who taxed even my neat fingers by the necessity for collecting his head furnishings daily into five tiny plaits tied with silk.

Not all these were personal companions; we bred dogs later and for a time sold them, but all got a full measure of tender care and consideration and the breeding was soon given up as we found we could not bear to sell our produce and see them go off to an unknown future. Those who wished to buy from us thought us cranks and having agreed to part with their money were bored or resentful at receiving endless instructions and having to undergo an apparently endless catechism as to the home and care they were prepared to offer.

In the world of dog shows too, though we had many good friends and incidentally were very successful, there were also some who thought us cranks. They resented our championship of the exhibits as sentient creatures and our unrestrained denunciation of certain inhuman practices and of those exhibitors who, provided a dog could win for them, thought it quite permissible to leave the shivering beast deserted and lying on a bed of scanty straw through the long winter nights of a 'three day' Crufts or Kennel Club show. I say 'we' said and did these things, for all our canine activities (and by that time all our other interests and pursuits) were shared, but I want to make it clear that in this, as in so much else, she was the initiator, the leader and, however little she realized it, the teacher. Since childhood I had loved animals, had revelled in the scanty opportunities afforded to a London child of country and farm life and had imposed my love of dogs, especially, upon my rather reluctant family. Since my marriage I had owned a number of dogs and they had always been cherished and well-cared for. Moreover I had inherited or acquired from my father a horror of killing and of all blood-sports. But it was John, and John alone who, without any conscious intention, taught me to appreciate the rights of animals and conferred on me the painful privilege of the 'seeing eye', until in the end I also could not fail to remark the underfed or over-loaded horse or ass, the chained or neglected dog, the un-tamed bird in the dirty, cruelly tiny cage. But before my eyes were cleansed, I remember once to my shame saying angrily: 'You spoil everything! We can never go any-where that you don't see some animal that makes you unhappy. . . .' And it is to the credit of her influence alone that I became in time as earnest as she was in the cause of the weaker brethren, willingly toiled half across Europe burdened with cages of rescued victims and on one occasion walked around Lisieux like a caricature of a Greuze maiden, clasping to my breast a dove that she had spotted on the fourth floor of a slum house. Having extracted it from a cage resembling a rat-trap, we were hunting the town for an ironmonger who could supply more suitable accom-modation.

All the same, I am glad to say that even our humani-tarianism had its light moments and I remember an occasion when we arrived at some seaside hotel for a holiday accom-panied by two dachshunds and a canary. By the time John had surveyed our bedroom and had decided upon a site where the canary would be safe from cats and on positions where the dogs could sleep immune from draughts, I was reduced to remarking: 'After all, darling, do remember that they did bring us. . . .'

To jump a long way backwards, I think Ladye occasion-ally felt something similar, for although she loved the dogs and willingly travelled with a tame Alexandrine parakeet called Lorim, there were two goldfish that were the bane of her existence. Not only did John insist upon their also travelling everywhere in a specially constructed zinc case, but she felt strongly that they must have unlimited exercise and insisted on their taking it in the bath, where Ladye complained of subsequently finding ants' eggs and less pleasant reminders of their activities.

I shall say more, later, of the animals she owned and loved; they were so much a part of her life, up to the very end, that they cannot be passed over briefly – but this particular digression seems to have carried me an unduly long way from Watergate Bay in 1915.

We all spent the following winter in London, and in common with other Londoners we gaped at the Zeppelins and later at the aeroplanes that passed over our heads. John was by then anxious to undertake some active war-work, but she was quite seriously ill for a time and when she recovered it was to nurse me through pneumonic tonsilitis and to realize that Ladye (was she perhaps subconsciously aware of the impending separation?) was surprisingly insistent that she would not be left alone. In view of the lingering aftermath of her accident John would not insist and she confined her war activities to visiting the wounded in St. Thomas' Hospital and serving in a canteen. Neither of them, as it happened, had any close friend or relation involved in the struggle, and they had therefore no deep personal anxiety.

On three occasions, during that winter and in early spring, John and I went out of London together for a few days. In late November she took me down to Malvern and I saw the White Cottage for the first time. Soon afterwards we spent some days together at the Wellington Hotel in Tunbridge

Wells and in early spring, Ladye not feeling up to the effort, I went alone with John to Malvern again where we stayed at the Hornyold Arms and superintended the handing over of the White Cottage to its new owners. Both John and Ladye were grieved at its sale, as they had been so happy there, had made the garden together and the whole place had many associations, but retrenchment had become imperative and it had to go. It was an unpretentious but very attractive little house of uncertain age, long and low and built upon the side of a hill so that the first floor as seen from the front became the garden level at the back. It had a verandah running the whole length of the back elevation and a series of photographs exist of Ladye and John, sitting and standing on this verandah, accompanied by Rufus, the collie, Claude, a large old-fashioned Yorkshire terrier, and Lorim, the Alexandrine parakeet.

But any regrets regarding the cottage were soon swept from our minds for in May 1916, with terrible suddenness, came tragedy and the blow that was again to alter the course of John's life. On May 10th John and I had arranged to spend the day at Maidenhead, bent on the inspection of a French bulldog puppy which, if it proved suitable, she was proposing to give me. The weather was lovely and so was Maidenhead, and, having left Ladye busy and contented preparing to sing that day at an afternoon party, we debated remaining for the night at Skindles and returning to London in the morning. I have always thanked God that we decided against it, for when I reached my London flat before dinner but rather later than we had intended, I heard Ladye's voice for the last time on this earth. Having returned from the party she rang me up to ask whether John was on her way home and I, having told her that this was the case, we laughed together when I also told her that, so far from having bought me a puppy, John had invested in a gangling untrained specimen for herself . . . Ladye's rueful comment being 'Not *another* dog!'

About an hour later the telephone rang again. This time it was John asking for my doctor's name and address as their own was not available. She seemed worried but quite collected and told me very briefly that Ladye, having dined normally and drunk a glass of red wine, had suddenly felt very unwell and was complaining of pins and needles all down one side. Of what this symptom portended John was as ignorant as I was myself. I gave the required address and as a matter of course hurried off to their hotel. By the time I got there, Ladye was unconscious. The cerebral haemorrhage was a gradual one, but it affected the speech centres from the first and though she lingered on until May 25th, showed that she recognized John and on one occasion managed to raise her hand to her lips and kiss it, she was never able to speak again.

John's grief was overwhelming and was intensified by remorse. She blamed herself bitterly and uncompromisingly that she had allowed her affection for me to trespass upon her exclusive devotion to Ladye, that she had brought me so closely into their home life, thereby as she thought, marring the happiness of Ladye's last months on earth . . . she saw no excuse for herself in the fact, fully realized by Ladye, of the twenty-four years' difference in their ages and her comparative youth. She even reproached herself for that last day at Maidenhead. She turned to me instinctively in her despair, as she was always, thank God, to turn to me in all trouble throughout her life, and yet, paradoxically, her desire for expiation was such that I think there was a time when, had she only considered herself, she would have put me out of her life and offered me up as a

54

sacrifice to loyalty. But even in the depths she was incapable at all times of considering herself alone, and there is proof of that in an incident during Ladye's last illness. Day and night John had sat beside her, awaiting what she knew to be the inevitable end but clinging to the hope that before it came there might be a momentary return to full consciousness that would allow her to speak of her deathless devotion and to receive absolution for any real or imagined shortcomings. But when, before the end, the doctor told her that consciousness could be induced by an injection, if it was for any reason desirable, she utterly refused to accept consolation for herself at the risk of rousing Ladye to possible pain . . . and she let her go in silence.

With the same generosity, she would not even scourge herself at my expense, since she realized that she had become the be-all and end-all of my life . . . and as often happens, her unselfishness had its reward. A friendship and companionship which at that time she continued chiefly for my sake, too numb with grief to feel any personal reaction, grew steadily and ripened between us until it became as precious, fulfilling and essential to her as ever it could be to me . . . until neither of us could have claimed to care more than the other or could have conceived that even death could divide us.

For a short time after Ladye's death, though we spent some hours together almost every day, we did not, at first, share a home. I had taken a furnished house, since demolished, in Royal Hospital Road (it was ancient, most attractive and quite abominably haunted) and John, for the time being, became a paying guest in her cousin Dorothy Clarke's house, No. 1 Swan Walk, a few yards away. It was a terribly unhappy time for us both and there seemed no light ahead. John was submerged by an all-pervading sorrow. I was torn by sympathy and by anxiety on her behalf and also desperately miserable at what looked like an almost total shipwreck of our happy relationship. When we met there were hours of mutual sympathy and understanding, but quite as many hours, at first, when we frayed each other's nerves.

I was not well; an old heart affection had recurred under the stress of anxiety and, partly with the idea that a change might do me good but partly in the hope that it might help us to a release of tension, John took me to an hotel at Llanberis in Wales. I remember that Rufus the Collie went with us. It was lonely and beautiful and we went to the top of Snowdon and trailed round Carnarvon Castle, with John nobly trying to be cheerful for my sake . . . but it was not a success.

She was seeing a good deal at the time of Ladye's only daughter, anxious in this respect to carry out what she knew to have been Ladye's wish, but it is seldom that such wishes bear posthumous fruit and this case proved no exception to the rule. She even took Lady Clarendon as her guest to St. Leonards but as the jealousy complex survived even death and John told me on her return that she had been freely entertained with thinly-veiled animadversions upon Ladye's mental and physical characteristics, that experiment was not repeated.

We gradually spent more and more time together, the fact being that not only was a fundamentally deep affection asserting its sway, but that also, in spite of all the elements that seemed to oppose it, I was the person who most completely understood her bereavement and to whom she could most easily talk of all that she had lost, of all that tormented her. Before very long another factor arose to cement our union. She developed measles and her cousin, who feared infection for her baby, practically turned her out at an hour's notice. There was a bed and an eager welcome waiting for her in my house and she remained there until she was able to move into a flat of her own at Cadogan Court, Draycott Avenue. She had signed the lease before Ladye's death and she kept it on till the end of the war, though latterly it was let furnished. While she lived there I would sleep there as often as not. Before long the air-raids became so serious that I gave up the London house and moved my child and her nurse to 'Grimston', a little furnished villa at Datchet, and John and I made common cause at Cadogan Court, frequently visiting the child at 'Grimston' and later at 'Swanmead', another furnished house in Datchet.

From that time onwards we shared a home, or rather a succession of homes, and were never apart for more than a few days (and that only, I think, four times) in the twenty-seven years that remained to her of earthly life.

We had also by that time begun to share a common interest and a very laborious investigation. We were already launched upon the intensive study of psychical phenomena, at which we worked systematically for a number of years, as is testified by various publications in the Proceedings of the Society for Psychical Research.

At the time of Ladye's death, war and consequent bereavements had aroused an unprecedented interest in the possibility of communication with the deceased and it was inevitable that someone should propose to John that a visit to a medium might result in consolation. Neither she, Ladye nor myself had ever taken the slightest interest in such matters and moreover we all belonged to a church that holds very strong views upon the inadvisability of such practices. In any case, what was proposed to us in the first instance was sheer, uncritical, credulous spiritualism. However, desperate cases grasp at desperate remedies, a medium recommended by a friend was visited, with disconcerting and, since the medium in question was mentally unstable, most unpleasant results. Neither of us was sufficiently unbalanced or uncritical to accept such phenomena as genuine, but by that time John had read quite a lot on the subject and she was still anxious to pursue her investigations in some more reliable manner.

Since her temperament was such that her demand for unequivocal proof kept pace with her desire for conviction, it was essential that our new start should be made under reliable guidance. And it was at that juncture that Sir Oliver Lodge published his book *Raymond* and renewed a statement which he had already made some years earlier to the effect that he was convinced of personal survival of bodily death and of the possibility of communication between the dead and the living.

This is the story of Radclyffe Hall and not a treatise on psychical or psychological controversy, and I am not proposing to discuss Sir Oliver's beliefs, but whatever may or may not have been their justification, at that time he certainly represented the highest scientific aspect of the subject and I decided, on John's behalf, to write to him for advice as to our next venture.

A most courteous reply led to us visiting the medium Mrs. Osborne Leonard, and to our undertaking investigation of her phenomena in the careful and critical manner recommended by Sir Oliver.

The measure of conviction we obtained is not a matter I propose to discuss just now. What was in any case of immense importance to John, in her desperate unhappiness, was that before very long her intelligent and cautious reports and comments had so impressed Sir Oliver that he asked for more and proceeded to train us relentlessly in the way we should go.

Very soon we were sitting regularly and frequently with Mrs. Leonard, were also testing other mediums, were employing a full-time secretary to type notes and reports, and John, with myself as collaborator and second in command, was launched upon an existence of regular and painstaking industry such as she had never before even dreamed of. The idle apprentice was metamorphosed by sorrow into someone who would work from morning to night and from night till morning, or travel half across England and back again to verify the most trifling detail.

Nor were our labours confined to our own investigations. Having, at Sir Oliver's suggestion, joined the Society for Psychical Research and thereby made the acquaintance of the scholars who had for so long directed its activities: Lord (then Sir Gerald) Balfour, Mrs. Henry Sidgwick, Mr. J. G. Piddington and others, we found ourselves preparing a paper which John read at a meeting of the Society, undertaking various subsidiary tasks, and concurrently to all this we undertook on Sir Oliver's behalf a special form of 'war work'. We dealt with a large proportion of the people who, being bereaved, wrote to him for information and assistance, we examined their circumstances and credentials and when we thought it advisable escorted them to sittings and acted as note-takers for them, reporting the results to Sir Oliver.

Looking back upon the uncertain and meagre personal harvest that we eventually reaped from all this arduous labour, I can only feel that, for us, it served its chief purpose in training John in that infinite capacity for taking pains that she had so signally lacked, that became so salient a characteristic of her methods in later life and brought her natural genius to complete fruition.

Of course, as Catholics, we were faced very early in our venture with the Church's veto upon all spiritualistic practices, but fortunately for us, just at that time, a very eminent scholar-priest published his opinion that those who were genuinely investigating these alleged phenomena with an open mind undertook a good and not an evil work. We approached him and having satisfied him that our minds were indeed open we continued our activities with his knowledge and approval, frequently discussing with him debatable and interesting phenomena . . . his also was essentially the open mind.

And, as a matter of fact, twenty-seven years of experience and study in these matters left us both, John and myself, still with . . . the open mind. We discussed the question shortly before her death and when we both knew that bodily separation was imminent and she asked me whether, when the time came, I should attempt to establish communication through a medium, I replied that I did not for a moment think so. I disliked the processes associated with such alleged communication through a third person and felt that my faith would be strong enough to sustain me until I could join her. I added, however, that most things were possible and that I might conceivably find myself so desperately unhappy that I would attempt even that expedient. Her reply was that, should I ever do so and should it prove possible, she from her side would, of course, do her utmost to respond. I then asked her: 'If it were the other way round and I were going and leaving you behind, what would *you* do? Would you go to Mrs. . . . ?' (And I mentioned a celebrated medium of acknowledged integrity.) Her answer was emphatic: 'No;

never. . . . The Communion of Saints would be enough for me.'

It has also been and will be enough for me during our temporary separation, and I have thought it worth while to set down here what were our measured conclusions on the question when we ourselves became most deeply involved.

Peace was declared and it found us established in our first unfurnished home: the first also of a series of homes of which the freehold or a very long lease was bought under the impression that we should remain in them for the rest of our lives. In this respect we both suffered from incurable optimism, and in any case we got an immense amount of fun out of our various ventures and the fun would not have been nearly so fulfilling if we had not at each fresh beginning been completely convinced that here at last we had discovered the perfect home for all the years to come and for our old age.

Our homes! Houses, flats, large and small, in town and country, in England and in Italy . . . each in its turn seemed ideal and in none of them did we remain longer than four years. Time and again we immersed ourselves gravely in preliminary discussions that heralded the next move. Gravely we agreed that we were only suited to a country life and dog breeding. With equal gravity, after a couple of years of rustication we concluded that what we wanted was a house very accessible to London and its activities. After a period of suburban experiment we (or shall we say John in this instance, but always with my loyal assent) rebelled at the constant journeys to and fro and decided that only urban life provided the necessary stimulus for her work. One home proved too big, another was definitely much too small and when circumstances at length took us to Florence, which we both loved dearly, we left our first flat after a year of gasping in pitiless Italian sunshine only to discover that the agreeably cool one that succeeded it had also definite disadvantages.

The coming of the Second World War found us discussing the conflicting attractions of the flat we had left in Florence and a villa we happened to have seen at Fiesole, and 1942 saw John hankering for an ancient dilapidated little house with its feet in the cold sea at Lynmouth. She liked the idea that at high tide and in stormy weather the waves beat against its walls! Truly it seems fortunate that in the country where I am going to meet her again we have been told that there are many mansions!

But to return to our first real home. It was a modern, pretentious and very ugly house at Hadley Wood, Middlesex, twelve miles from London, with the absurd name of 'Chip Chase' and a façade that included a turret with rough-cast battlements. We were quite aware that it suggested the forts that used to appear at Hamley's toyshop in the Christmas season. But we were also aware that, as a consequence of the war, it was almost impossible to make repairs or alterations and that our mock castle, which belonged to a rich industrial magnate, contained, for a comparatively reasonable price, every comfort and convenience that our hearts could desire. That price also included carpets, curtains and fixtures, the selection of which the owner, wisely mistrusting his own taste, had entrusted to Burnetts of Covent Garden. The house, moreover, was a stone's throw from the beautiful Hadley Woods.

And so John and I thumbed our noses at jeers and she bought a ninety-nine years' lease of Chip Chase and we enjoyed our first orgy of selecting and discarding the furniture she already possessed and of hunting for and buying the early oak which she had always loved and which she

Una Troubridge at the time of her first meeting with Radclyffe Hall.

Radclyffe Hall the year 'The Well of Loneliness' was published.
1928.

taught me to love and to understand. We had a glorious time, the first of many, and a great deal of the furniture I now possess evokes those wonderful thrills that perennially accompanied the discovery of something really beautiful and unquestionably genuine. Presently we moved in, with a personal maid, four house servants, a gardener and a gardener's boy and were we comfortable and were our supercilious friends only too willing to visit us and enjoy that comfort! There was a glass-tiled, marble-flagged bathroom with a glass-enclosed bath and masses of chromium-plated intestines that in itself was a special exhibit. . . . And, joking apart, the rooms as seen from the inside were beautifully proportioned and, with our furniture, very attractive.

There was a pleasant little office where the psychical work was done and where the secretary had her habitat, and a big study for John opening on to the garden. But the drawing-room seemed at first superfluous. It soon proved to have its uses all the same, for we laid linoleum, fitted it with wooden partitions and commissioned it as a home for our growing kennel of griffons.

It was an interesting and pleasant life. Plenty of work needing close application; reports that must be so adequate and so accurate that they did not return to us from Sir Oliver or from the trinity of scholars at Fisher's Hill with slightly satirical notes and queries. Regular sittings with Mrs. Osborne Leonard and with any other medium who aroused the interest of the Society for Psychical Research. Visits to and from members of that Society and particularly from members of its Council (it was during our time at Chip Chase that John was co-opted to that Council). And on one occasion a visit from a young woman whose interest for the Society lay in the fact that she was liable

without warning to become one of two other personalities!
This she proceeded to do at Chip Chase at frequent intervals.

Then there were, of course, the dogs; John had given
me a red dachshund bitch of matchless beauty: Champion
Brandesburton Caprice, the holder of seven challenge cer-
tificates, re-christened by us Thora the Fairest of Women.
She was as hysterical as she was devoted. Later, she crept
into *The Forge* under the name of 'Sieglinde', though some
of that lady's adventures were imaginary.

The first griffon was mine: Fitz-John Minnehaha (we
had by then invested in a Kennel Club prefix), alias Tinkie,
a Brabançonne weighing three-and-a-quarter pounds, a
wonderful specimen but ineligible for show, having been
born a 'war-baby'. Her charms were such, however, that
she ushered in the Kennel . . . we took to breeding and
showing griffons rough and smooth and got a lot of pleasure
out of it, though the difficulties were such and the casualties
so frequent that like many other people in that breed we
gave it up and subsequently only entertained griffons as
pets.

John's personal dogs at Chip Chase were Olaf, a blue
Dane, huge and docile and devoted, who went into a series
of epileptic fits at twelve months old and had to be shot by
the vet in the garden. . . . I can suddenly remember John's
face as we sat waiting for the sound of that shot. . . . She
also had a tiny Blenheim spaniel, Prudence. Prudence remained alive but as she grew up proved to lack discrimina-
tion in her affections, or rather to prefer any lap to any individual. She was transferred to a lady who was ready to
offer a perpetual lap.

But the end of Chip Chase came after about two years.
Not only were we bored by the much-advertised 'twelve
miles to the Marble Arch' that were to have been such a

trifle, but which were a dreary penance of tramlines and traffic, not only was the neighbourhood suburban in the extreme, but the size of the house and the number of the servants were devouring income which we felt could be spent to better advantage.

Like Hilary and Susan Brent in *The Forge,* between one day and another we decided that what we wanted was a small house in London accessible to our friends, to theatres, and dog shows, and so economical in upkeep that we could afford to leave it if and when we wished to travel. And so, after an interim period of hotels, of Italy and of furnished houses, John bought No. 9 Sterling Street in Knights-bridge, just off Montpelier Square. Our staff was reduced to three and no gardeners, we stored such furniture as absolutely refused to be pulled, pushed or poured into our new abode (it was a freehold this time), and tried desperately to believe that we were comfortable. We were already becoming adept at counting our domiciliary blessings and also, if I may be forgiven a mixed metaphor, at ignoring rocks ahead.

It must be emphasized that our illusion in this case was favoured by the fact that although a great deal of work was in progress it was not then creative work. It had never occurred to either of us that a time was coming for John when quietness and seclusion would be essential to inspira-tion and when a sudden interruption might frustrate the output of many hours. The psychical records were only a matter of application and of careful accuracy, guests could be denied the door when we were dictating notes to the typist in the back part of our sitting-dining room, and the typist herself could be banished to a bedroom for copying and correcting her work.

So we started the era of Sterling Street confidently, even

if it was rather difficult to move about, if doors had had to be rehung to admit out-size furniture (old oak tends to be large) and if we had to eat our meals and entertain our friends sitting along one side of a refectory table, facing the wall. In spite of being unduly crowded, it was attractive. We had the communicating bedrooms that were dear to our conviviality and a delightful small gothic table and settle at the foot of my bed where we could, and did, have breakfast together. It was well-heated and got such sunshine as England provided and was near Harrods' stores for us and the park for the dogs. Thora was dead but we had Thorgils of Tredholt, another red dashshund bought by John at a Brighton dog show. He became a big winner and was presently joined by Wotan who as Champion Fitz-John Wotan helped to make dashshund history. He was a liver-and-tan, seen from the car by John in a side street in Shepherds Bush and bought for me from an old woman who had bred him. We got him registered without pedigree at the Kennel Club. He swept the benches and beat every dog he met but one (and in that case the judge was so openly doubtful that the rival was never allowed to risk a reversal of judgment). He sired seventy-three puppies during his first year at stud and gave me a passionate and exacting adoration that made my life a burden! I do not think I ever possessed so devoted or so selfish a dog! Fortunately town life disagreed with him and eventually he had to be pensioned off in the country. To this day I meet his unmistakable descendants in all kinds of unexpected places.

But before we settled into Sterling Street there was one great experience. We went to Florence together for the first time. We had both of us visited it and loved it in the past, but that was a very different thing from discovering all its joys and beauties in the company we both liked better than any in the world: that of each other. We spent an autumn, winter and early spring at the Hotel Albion on the Lung'Arno Acciaiuoli, looking across at the lovely houses of the Borgo San Jacopo reflected in the waters of the Arno. We watched them at sunrise, at noon and in the evening and when their windows glowed softly golden in a misty green twilight . . . and I have just learned that the Germans destroyed them before they left the city.

It was in 1921 that we were there, when Communism was rampant, atheistic slogans chalked up on every wall and the early Fascists, already too strong for total suppression, had been forbidden to carry arms. We would see bands of them swinging along the streets, many of them boys of fifteen and sixteen, wearing the black fez with its pendant tassel and its death's head device and 'armed' only with a cutting whip fastened by a thong to their wrists: the *manganello*.

But despite prohibitions they bore other arms at night. We would be woken by the sound of reports across the river in the San Frediano Communist quarter followed by the insistent ringing of a small bell. Questioning of the chambermaid in the morning would elicit that the reports were *colpi di rivoltella,* and on being asked about the bell she answered simply: '*Misericordia, signore. . . .*'

The movement at that time was still chiefly associated with Gabriele d'Annunzio, who was actually its founder. Medals were sold on the Ponte Vecchio bearing his head and on the reverse the Fascist war cry: '*Éya, éya, éya, alalà.*' But another name was already becoming familiar; another star was rising.

One day as we leaned out of the window of our room at the hotel we saw crowds hurrying by and coming also from other directions towards the junction of the Ponte alla Santa Trinita and the Via Tornabuoni. I called down to someone below to ask the reason for the commotion and was told: 'It is Benito Mussolini who has arrived at Santa Maria Novella and is coming to the bridge to speak to the people.' I was desperately anxious to sally forth to see and to listen, but John was adamant: I was to stay indoors. It was my Irish blood yearning for a free fight. I should get injured and embarrass my Italian friends by becoming an International Incident. . . . To this day I wish that I had been more insistent or that she had yielded.

But there were more peaceable distractions available in Florence. We were neither of us constitutional sightseers and went to see only such pictures and sculptures as we already knew and loved, but we got to know the real Florence very thoroughly; the Florence that is so beautiful that Or San Michele, the Mercato Nuovo and the Porcellino, the Loggia dei Lanzi and the Palazzo Vecchio are mere everyday incidents. We also got to know its shops and its food, but of the latter only one memory is very clear. Peasant-baked bread in the shape of a small wreath, which we bought straight from the oven in a cellar near the Ponte Vecchio; cool-tasting unsalted bread which we devoured in our bedroom with plenty of sweet fresh butter bearing the stamp of the Florentine Lily.

Four things remain to recall that happy time. The Fascist medal of d'Annunzio, jewelled cuff-links which I bought for John at Settepassi on the Ponte Vecchio. A big sapphire ring which she gave me and which I always wear and a treasure which I discovered by chance in a shabby little shop in the Via della Vigna Nuova. A tre-cento reproduction in miniature of the Volto Santo of Lucca cast in bronze with enamelled eyes. Its beauty was apparent to the most casual glance and we bought it for an absurdly small sum. It was only later when I cleaned it that I discovered that its shoes were silver and its crown and adornments of pure, yellow gold.

But Sterling Street, which we left so soon and so gladly (it was really a most uncomfortable little house and we never regretted it), had one claim to fame, for it was while we were living there – though actually while we were on holiday at Lynton in North Devon – that John made the most important decision of her life. We were staying, as on former occasions, at the Lynton Cottage Hotel and one evening, while we were at dinner, sitting at the end of the long room, we watched a couple of fellow guests making their way to their table: a small, wizened old lady and an elderly woman who was quite obviously her maiden daughter. The latter was carrying a shawl and a footwarmer and clutched a bottle of medicine. She fussed for several minutes round the old lady, putting the footwarmer under her feet, the shawl round her shoulders and inquiring if she felt warm enough and not too warm before she herself attempted to sit down. And John said to me in an undertone: 'Isn't it ghastly to see these unmarried daughters who are just unpaid servants and the old people sucking the very life out of them like octopi!' And then as suddenly: 'I shall write it. I shall write Heinemann's book for him and I shall call it *Octopi*.'

And so she began her first novel: it was only on the eve of publication that, at my suggestion, the title became *The Unlit Lamp*.

It took her two years to write it, for from the very beginning she was not a regular worker. Never for her the steady output, at fixed hours, of so many words a day. It is true that she did not at first work at night; her bad habits grew with the years. But from the beginning she had hours and days of urgent, fertile inspiration, alternating with days and hours of blank, arid inability to string two words together. From the first her work was of the kind that comes only as it listeth, a fact that she was not always prepared to accept. I have seen her almost unaffected by incredibly long spells of continuous writing and I have also seen her grey with exhaustion when, determined to dispose of some situation, to complete some section or chapter, she has wrestled vainly, hour after hour, against an inspirational blackout.

Knowing the devastating effects on her health and nerves of such fruitless battling I have many times implored her to desist, to wait until the spirit really moved her, and occasionally I would prevail, but much more often I would be told I was a fool for my pains . . . though later, when mournfully but firmly destroying the results of her persistence she would generously admit that I had been right!

Whether she felt inspired or not, her method of work never varied. She never herself used a typewriter, in fact she never learned to type and the mere thought of dictating her inspiration to a typist filled her with horror. She always said that the written word was to her an essential preliminary and she wrote her work with pen or pencil, very illegibly, generally mis-spelt and often without punctuation. Sometimes she wrote in manuscript books but, especially in later years, often on loose sheets of sermon paper or indeed on paper of any kind, and to this day I will find scraps covered with sentences and sometimes discover 'try outs' on a bit of blotting paper or an old cardboard box. Occasionally she would have a spasm of determination to produce a sightly and presentable manuscript and a laborious effort would be made; spelling was to her always an insoluble mystery, and she was ludicrously distressed by this deficiency (which, incidentally, is by no means infrequent among talented people). She was quite seriously ashamed of it and would constantly ask me to inspect letters she had written and insist on re-writing them if I reluctantly pointed out mistakes. It was quite incurable; however often she would ask for the spelling of a particular word she would always revert to her (doubly) original versions. These sometimes varied but on the whole were fairly consistent and became very familiar to me with the passing years. She got some consolation from the discovery that she shared this affliction with Stephen Vincent Benét, who told her that he had refused a very large sum from a public museum for the manuscript of *John Brown's Body,* as he would not allow his fantastic spelling to humiliate him posthumously in the eyes of posterity.

The first draft accomplished, the next step would be to ask me to read her what she had written. Luckily I had so long been familiar with her writing that the wildest scrawl presented little difficulty to me. In fact, I sometimes deciphered hieroglyphics that defeated the ingenuity of their author. . . . I would read and read again as often as she desired and as I read she would dictate alterations and corrections and these I would put down and incorporate in the next reading. (This explains the fact that my handwriting appears on some of her manuscripts.)

If she was satisfied with what she had done, the next stage would be dictation to a typist who was trained to her particular method of dictation. This involved never 'tapping' while she spoke or while she was reflecting. For as she dictated she continued to polish and the typist had always to be prepared to 'X' out at demand any word or sentence and continue her script with the substituted amendment.

That script was again read aloud by me, but generally after further correction by John, and so the stages would move on to re-typing, to further readings and further correction until the result satisfied her and reached the goal of the 'publisher's copy', which she insisted should be spotless and practically without corrections.

I have known a chapter worked on for weeks on end. I have often read one aloud a score of times and I learned to read so closely to punctuation that she knew by my timing whether she had put down a semi-colon or a comma. Never can any writer have taken more patient pains than did this erstwhile idle apprentice.

There was immense interest for me in my share of her labours, as I would find myself always the first to read and to hail the beautiful prose which was later to delight so many; to follow the intricate weaving of those large tapestries upon which she preferred to work.

There was also need for the exercise of tact and for the not infrequent acting of a drama which was essential to her processes. After a day or night spent like Jacob, wrestling with the angel of her own uninspired obstinacy, she would hand me the resulting manuscript with an excellent simulation of self-confidence and command me to read it aloud. This I would solemnly proceed to do with the best imitation I could produce of approval and appreciation. But in spite of my efforts there would be a growing flatness in my voice that infuriatingly confirmed her own infallible judgment; and having been asked whether I was tired and told that I was reading abominably and sometimes informed that my ineptitude was ruining the beauty of what I read, the manuscript would be snatched from my hands and torn to shreds or thrown into the fire. Physically and mentally exhausted, black depression would overwhelm her. She had seen the last of her inspiration, she would never write again. . . . What she had written was as dead as Queen Anne, it would shame a child of seven . . . why had she ever imagined she could write? Nothing like this had ever happened to her before . . . and so on and so on until, in spite of chronic insomnia, sleep would come, and days perhaps of stagnation and recuperation. Days also when she would give way to my persuasion, and, chiefly for my sake, would agree to a 'first night', to a meal at a restaurant, to seeing some of our friends (and would incidentally thoroughly enjoy these distractions herself); when the dogs would move into the foreground and their grooming and exercising would be taken over from the maid; when she would indulge in housework and in strenuous polishing of our collection of old oak (at this period of our peregrinations there was no scope for the gardening which she always loved), and then, as suddenly as it had left her, one day inspiration would blaze out once more.

There was another recurrent aspect of her literary labours: the books that she herself well knew would never see publication; that were without salient merits and served merely as trolleys to carry her from a fallow period to one of renewed production.

There were several of these, but one in particular was re-written at least three times, an apparent waste of energy extending each time to some twenty-five thousand words. But it acted as the baptist to what she herself (and I also) always considered her best book: *The Master of the House,* and also to *The Sixth Beatitude.*

In the case of the 'trolley' books the drama was the same as in that of her briefer bouts of spiritual dryness, but it was prolonged and much more elaborate. After she had finished a book and corrected the proofs there would be a time of happy, contented indolence; of quiet consciousness of work well done, of holidays in the country, at the seaside or abroad (we hardly ever stayed in other people's houses, much preferring our own independence). For her an orgy of being read aloud to by me. This reading aloud was in any case a constant feature of all times, one of our chief pleasures and her chief relaxation. But when she was engaged upon her own work she barred the reading of good English novels, lest they might affect her own style, and our programme was restricted to biographies, history and memoirs, French books of any description and detective fiction, in which she frankly revelled. I would read to her endlessly and many times I thanked God that my voice had once been trained and never seemed to fail me. I would read by day and often by night in an effort to exorcize her constitutional sleeplessness. When we went away together to an hotel the first things to be unpacked were at least a dozen books of every description. I would have borrowed or bought them on various recommendations and have glanced through them provisionally or have read them myself.

My star-turn was when we lay on twin beds at the Osborne Hotel in Paris while I read her for eight hours on end Stephen Vincent Benét's *John Brown's Body*. On that occasion even my voice went on strike!

But these periods of enjoyment had their inevitable sequel. One day she would awake with a faint feeling of anxiety and presently that anxiety would find expression in an apparently casual remark to the effect that it was now some time since she had finished her last book. Even while I made an equally casual reply, reminding her of how desperately hard she had worked and of the exhaustion from which she had afterwards suffered, I knew that the halcyon days were over and that the curtain had rung up for the usual performance.

That faint anxiety of hers would grow like Jack's beanstalk until it overshadowed every other consideration. Why was she still without an idea in her head? Was she never going to be able to write another book? She was getting no younger and her output might be over . . . she had not begun to write till maturity. Never had she known so prolonged a period of stagnation! Was I sure that the last book had been really first-class! After all, there had been some adverse reviews. Come to think of it, she couldn't remember many good ones! Did I remember such and such a criticism? Was it really worth while her writing at all? And yet again and again and again: why was she without the ghost of an inspiration? Head by head I would tackle this Hydra; infinitely pitiful of what she endured but perfectly confident of the ultimate issue, and almost invariably her misery would seek relief in the gestation or resurrection of a trolley book and the curtain rise upon the second act.

It would all be undertaken with the utmost gravity and the Lord knows she suffered enough in the process! Silence and concentration and all the customary routine would ensue. Long hours of grinding out chapter after chapter of well-constructed prose lacking the breath of life. Long hours of listening to my reading of the same, perpetual assurances (for her own reassurance) that what she was writing surpassed all that had preceded it. My assent demanded and duly supplied while neither of us was ever deceived for a moment. Writing, reading, dictating, correcting, typing and retyping, and I would wonder wearily how long it must continue. Fury at times at my alleged lack of appreciation, but a half-hearted fury aimed chiefly at herself. One by one the chapters would be completed: the eighth, the ninth, the tenth, the eleventh. . . .

Then one day a morning of feverish concentration as I sat patiently beside her in careful silence waiting to put up a creditable reading of chapter twelve. A few sheets handed to me without any comment:

'In a quiet curve of the coast of Provence, in a stretch of that coast which before the war was seldom if ever visited by strangers, lies the small sea-port town of Saint-Loup-sur-Mer, cleansed by strong winds and purified by sunshine.'

There was no more need of reassurance on either side, the drama was over and the Holy Spirit had descended, and I read her the first chapter of *The Master of the House*.

It was five years later that that scene was repeated exactly. It was the day on which we moved from a flat in St. Martin's Lane which we had joyfully furnished a couple of years earlier. The trolley book had on this occasion progressed even further; it had, if I remember rightly, been entirely re-written and its name for us both was deathly weariness.

John was sitting at her immense desk surrounded by chaos. That desk and our chairs were the only remaining furniture in a flat that was actually in the process of 'removal'.

Through sheer cussedness, as it seemed, she had elected to choose that morning for work, and to add yet more weariness to that moribund book. But I was well-trained and I certainly knew better than to protest, especially as on this occasion she very soon desisted. Moreover she was amiable and definitely apologetic:

'I know I'm the limit; I don't know how you endure me! But will you read me this and tell me what you think of it.' Only one sheet this time and the removal could proceed:

76

'Hannah Bullen stood staring seaward. Romney Marsh stretched out between her and the sea, more than two miles of greyish-green marsh with cattle upon it, sheep and strong steers – for a long time ago the sea had left Rother.'

And no more was heard of that unhappy trolley book. Packed away among the manuscripts of the books that are so familiar is the definitive typescript of that perennial hobby-horse – it will never be published and I suppose I should destroy it. Actually it contained one fragment of inspiration which did see publication as a short story: *Fräulein Schwartz.* It did also embody an excellent theme, but it was not destined to join the works of Radclyffe Hall. Yet somehow I feel a reluctance to burn it; it has already borne the heat of the day.

But, talking of destruction, there was one respect in which I trained John and repeatedly read the riot act until she ceased to transgress. In the early days of her writing, when dissatisfied with a piece of work after a first trial reading, she would sit down to re-model it nearer to her heart's desire. And sometimes she would be perfectly right and the second version would surpass the first. But it occasionally happened that her dissatisfaction was unjustified; was born perhaps of a mood induced by exhaustion and overwork, and that when I came to read and she to hear her revised version, our eyes would meet and she would say . . . 'I know what you're thinking. The first one was better. . . .' and I would reply: 'Of course it was. Let me read it to you again : where is it ?' Guiltily she would look at me and confess that she had destroyed it. If it had been torn up it meant only patient reconstruction of the fragments in the waste-paper basket, but sometimes the flames had already had their way.

There came a day when after such a disaster I exacted a

solemn promise that never, never again would she destroy anything until we had finally examined it together and she had confirmed her verdict of destruction, and I am able to record that she kept that promise.

I have related how she at last decided to write 'Heinemann's book', and the fact that it took her two years to write it. None of her books was to have a peaceful career and *The Unlit Lamp* was no exception. She met and conquered all the difficulties of her inexperience, sustained by the memory of a great publisher's praise. And before the book was half completed came the news of Mr. Heinemann's unexpected death; she had waited too long to fulfil his prophecy.

His firm had the first offer of the book and declined to publish it, as did nine other well-known publishers. They were unanimous in declaring that it was a work of merit, but too long and too depressing to find a public, especially as the book of an unknown novelist. I. A. R. Wylie and J. D. Beresford, who had agreed to read it, were not encouraging, but from somewhere or someone there came a suggestion that if John could write a much shorter, light novel and could get it accepted, it might facilitate the publication of *The Unlit Lamp*.

Depressed and discouraged, she yet held to her conviction that *The Unlit Lamp* was worthy of success. If it needed a herald, then it should have it and she wrote *The Forge* in less than five months. It was published by Arrowsmith in 1924 and was very well received; they were eager for more, but they had firmly classified her as a humorous writer and had no use at all for *The Unlit Lamp*.

If I went into all her publishing vicissitudes I might become libellous as well as boring. It suffices to say that *The Unlit Lamp* was published by Cassell in 1924 and established her reputation and that after she had put paid to Arrowsmith with *A Saturday Life,* she was able in 1926 to give Newman Flower *Adam's Breed.*

Adam's Breed. The first I heard of it was at the Pall Mall restaurant, which was at that time rather a favourite haunt of ours. In the middle of a pleasant *tête-à-tête* luncheon John became abstracted and inattentive. Her eye was following our obsequious waiter and presently she said to me with quiet decision, 'I am going to write the life of a waiter who becomes so utterly sick of handling food that he practically lets himself die of starvation.'

Newman Flower wrote of *Adam's Breed* that it was the finest book that had been submitted to him in twenty years, that he was proud to publish it but did not expect it to sell. It won John the James Tait Black Memorial Prize, the Femina Vie Heureuse Prize and the American Eichelberger gold medal. It sold twenty-seven thousand copies in the first three weeks and is still selling steadily after nineteen years. It is one of the books that has come to stay. It was translated into German, Dutch, Norwegian, Swedish, Italian and I cannot remember what other languages. Though it criticized the Italians they loved it dearly and accepted the criticism as just.

It was in *Adam's Breed,* when it was published, in 1927, that a dedication first made its appearance that was subsequently repeated in every book that she wrote. That dedication: 'To Our Three Selves', that has aroused so much curiosity among her readers. Many were the letters that reached her from all parts of the world, asking for the identity of the Three Persons alluded to, but during her lifetime John smiled and kept her own counsel in the matter; she vouchsafed no explanation, and, at her wish, I also held my peace.

However, since her death it has come to my knowledge that the dedication has continued to stimulate curiosity and that speculation has in some cases led to erroneous conclusions, and I think the time has come to reveal the very simple solution of the mystery:

The Three Selves referred to in the dedication were Ladye, who had encouraged her first efforts in prose and of whose continued interest she was firmly convinced; myself, whose glad and humble service to her talent she chose thus to acknowledge and honour and . . . Radclyffe Hall, since, generous as she was in her tribute to Ladye's influence and to my service, she could not deny that the books were her own creation.

I could write an entire book about John collecting copy, for whenever and wherever she sought it, I went with her. Sometimes it was I who enabled her to collect it. I it was who discovered the macaroni factory in Old Compton Street and introduced her as an eccentric signorina who wished to inspect it. Soho, of course, she knew in her bones, and *The Doric* was born after an exhaustive tour of the underground regions of the Berkeley.

We followed Gian Luca step by step to the New Forest and I am not likely to forget our hunt for that charcoal burner; we trudged and waded in abominable weather and found him at last; almost, it seemed, by chance, and she listened for hours while he expounded his lore.

I remember that I beguiled a part of the time by extracting a sheep-tick from his kitten's ear!

Her final exploit in regard to *Adam's Breed* she performed without me under the escort of Dr. Brontë, the pathologist. He took her to visit a public mortuary so that she could verify details of procedure and it was not until at least three weeks had elapsed that she revealed to me that its only occupant had been a baby recently dead of diphtheria! . . .

Adam's Breed was another case of an altered title and here again Lynton comes into the picture. We were once more staying at the Cottage Hotel when Newman Flower put through a trunk call; he had been considering the original title: *Food*, and had made up his mind that he could not digest it. John was too agitated to grasp what he said, but I hung on until I heard him protesting that with such a title the book would be still-born. . . .

'It's bound to be mistaken for a cookery book', he wailed. Time was short and a title had to be found, and once more I displayed my solitary talent. Firmly rejecting John's frenzied suggestions, I ransacked the local Smith's for sources of inspiration and ended by finding what we required in Kipling's *Tomlinson*: 'I'm all 'oer-sib to Adam's Breed that I should mock your pain.' And what is more I still think it a most excellent title!

And since I am busy just here blowing my own trumpet, let me add that I also christened . . . *The Well of Loneliness, The Master of the House,* and *The Sixth Beatitude.*

It was after the success of *Adam's Breed* that John came to me one day with unusual gravity and asked for my decision in a serious matter: she had long wanted to write a book on sexual inversion, a novel that would be accessible to the general public who did not have access to technical treatises. At one time she had thought of making it a 'period' book, built round an actual personality of the early nineteenth century. But her instinct had told her that in any case she must postpone such a book until her name was made; until her unusual theme would get a hearing as being the work of an established writer.

It was her absolute conviction that such a book could only be written by a sexual invert, who alone could be qualified by personal knowledge and experience to speak on behalf of a misunderstood and misjudged minority.

It was with this conviction that she came to me, telling me that in her view the time was ripe, and that although the publication of such a book might mean the shipwreck of her whole career, she was fully prepared to make any sacrifice except – the sacrifice of my peace of mind.

She pointed out that in view of our union and of all the years that we had shared a home, what affected her must also affect me and that I would be included in any condemnation. Therefore she placed the decision in my hands and would write or refrain as I should decide.

I am glad to remember that my reply was made without so much as an instant's hesitation: I told her to write what was in her heart, that so far as any effect upon myself was concerned, I was sick to death of ambiguities, and only wished to be known for what I was and to dwell with her in the palace of truth.

Then and there she set to work on *The Well of Loneliness*.

But long before this Sterling Street was forgotten. After Italy came a period spent in furnished houses. There was one in Trevor Square, Knightsbridge, where we endured that curiously unendurable phenomenon that occasionally comes to England, a heat wave. Another in North Terrace, South Kensington, where sewer rats the size of rabbits proved to be sharing our tenancy. I remember that the house agent questioned our veracity and that when one of the intruders obligingly died in the kitchen I arranged him neatly in a shoe-box and posted him to the gentleman in question. There was a melancholy furnished flat in Kensington Palace Mansions and then another freehold; no, it was a lease that would outlast everybody, at 37 Holland Street, near the Carmelites in Church Street, Kensington.

And of course there was always at intervals 'dear abroad'. After the first journey to Italy we often crossed that abominable Channel which John rather enjoyed and which I braved because of what lay beyond it. She was invariably merciful in this respect and always saw that I was segregated in a private cabin in which, fortified by a dry martini cocktail (and by a second in mid-channel if the weather proved capricious), I would await in panic the seasickness that never materialized. While she humoured my phobia she would often point out that I would arrive at Calais unscathed and with a healthy colour on days when she had wrestled with impending disaster. But as a matter of fact she was an excellent sailor. She had occasional yearnings for a long sea voyage and sometimes distressed me by pointing out that my inability to share this yearning had erased that pleasure from her scheme of existence. I always replied that I would follow her anywhere, but I could not contemplate seafaring with pleasure.

But the Channel horrors at any rate were quickly over and then we could both settle down to their reward. Luncheon on the Paris train, and such a luncheon as it was in those days, ending up with the invariable tower of bombe glacée and with the coffee splashed into the thick pale-blue cups; and Paris itself, which we 'discovered' together. She already knew it but had never lived there and since it had for her no special associations we built up those associations together and came to know it well and to love it dearly. We also built up a circle of friends who always welcomed our arrival warmly and eagerly added to the pleasure of our visits: first and foremost Romaine Brooks, the painter of memorable canvases, and Natalie Barney (who lives in *The Well of Loneliness* as Valérie Seymour), The Duchesse de Clermont Tonnerre, Adrien Mirtil (who also figured in it, slightly

83

idealized, as the gentle and learned Jew) and the ever enchanting Colette, whose genius we revered while we revelled in her rare personality. Most of our visits to Paris were punctuated by the gift of another of her books. I have them all with those witty dedications for which she seemed never to lack inspiration. . . . Yes; Paris was always beloved and always new, always a signal for carefree enjoyment. It became peculiarly 'ours' and until the summer of 1926, when she was actually beginning to write the book, nobody was less aware than John that she was absorbing copy for *The Well of Loneliness*.

We had in the early days and after some uncomfortable experiments our own hotels, the little Osborne in the rue St. Roch, and later the Pont Royal in the rue du Bac, and we discovered and patronized the Vert Galant, that little riverside restaurant near the Palais de Justice where one ate and drank most admirably, upstairs or downstairs, and could entertain one's friends, as we very often did, in delightful little rooms with lunette windows looking out on to the Seine.

We went to many churches; to St. Étienne du Mont where Ste. Geneviève lies in her golden shrine and those exquisite twisted stairways lead one closer to heaven; to the Sacré Coeur, of course, which, like Stephen Gordon, we both loved but which was, it must be admitted, difficult of access, and more and more often to the unaesthetic Madeleine to which we were both drawn by the always beautiful music. In any case John had a passion for the Madeleine which had nothing to do with artistic appreciation. She would sometimes murmur to me during Mass: 'You do love it, don't you?' and closing my eyes to shut out the sculptural atrocities of the high altar I would murmur back quite truthfully that I did. Sometimes we descended to that shabby little chamber of horrors in the crypt where the authorities have bestowed such cheap or damaged statues of the saints as are not considered worthy of a place above. We would buy votive candles from the practical-minded attendant, especially for St. Expedit, who, we had been told, was able to ensure us a calm Channel crossing. Observing the destination of our candles the attendant once remarked: '*Ses clients sont d'habitude très satisfaits.*'

Bagnoles de l'Orne saw us at irregular intervals, for John the humanitarian was reaping the harvest sown by John the sportsman. A vein injured long ago in hunting began to cause anxiety and we went to Bagnoles so that she could take the baths. We became very fond of the dull little burg where the baths (which I also took) were pleasant enough and the unconquerable sleepiness that followed them delightful. Books we took with us, of course, as usual, and enticed the wild birds to join us in our bedroom. The chaffinches would bring their babies to see us and would feed them from the crop as we lay and watched them.

There was an unsuccessful visit to Monte Carlo, undertaken by John partly as an 'aftercure' and partly because I had never seen the Riviera. We went there '*hors saison*' and were very unhappy. It was before the evolution of a summer season and we found a desert of dusty streets and shuttered shops. Although years had elapsed since Ladye's death and John had thought herself able to face the past, the wound of her bereavement seemed to open afresh and no effort could dispel her abysmal depression. We had made up our minds to beat a retreat when one night she suddenly became violently ill. Whether it was food poisoning or a virulent chill, the results were such that I was panic-striken. The hotel people were as unsympathetic as only the French can be at their worst and offered no assistance in getting a doctor. Moreover I was well aware that the sanitation was fantastic. The lavatory ventilated into the bedroom and necessary repairs had not been forthcoming, and I was therefore doubly uneasy as to the possible origins of the illness.

The English doctor whom I finally located immediately plugged in morphia to stop the sickness and as soon as she was relatively able to travel we risked a return to Paris and civilization.

On arrival in Paris we were met by another manifestation of French character. If Monte Carlo was empty, Paris was full, attending the Salon de l'Automobile, and when we arrived at the Osborne Hotel, to which I had telephoned from Monte Carlo, the proprietor informed us calmly that he had no vacant rooms. He did not deny the fact of promised reservations but remarked that these had been *'seulement par téléphone'*. . . .

I remember trailing round Paris in a taxi, with John exhausted and barely convalescent, clutching as usual the inevitable dog (a griffon bitch not destined to survive quarantine), while eight hotels in succession refused us hospitality. At the Continental the porter went so far as to run out to our taxi, before it had pulled up, to inform us that they were full and already had a waiting list. . . . There are times when the most confirmed British globe-trotters would give the earth to be back in England!

But eventually we had luck at the Hotel Pont Royal, quiet and pleasant in the rue du Bac, and there in a bedroom converted into a study, John wrote much of *The Well of Loneliness*. It was one of three communicating rooms and we were happy enough there for several months. True, we shared a chronic dislike of hotel food, but luckily we also shared a passion for 'café complets' and I should not like to say how many thousand of these we consumed in the course of our peregrinations. We always stipulated when arranging 'terms' to be allowed a café complet in the place of a meal. . . .

We have sat together before countless trays, in England and in every part of Europe we have visited, and among the details that live in my memory is the shape and flavour of an endless succession of rolls, good, bad and indifferent, that we have broken together in various countries: the bread of the communion of perfect companionship.

It was in Paris that we bought the unforgettable Raton. She was a 'petite Brabançonne' just imported from Brussels and I bought her for John in the rue de Ponthieu. She was eight months old and weighed exactly one kilo; her ears were cropped, her head was the size and colour of a tangerine and she was one of the best griffons I have ever beheld. She opened the ball at luncheon by biting John; from her lap she had tried to get into her plate. Very soon afterwards she became my property. John said she was too small to carry and that she never knew whether she was carrying her or not. She fought every step of her education and I thought she would never consent to go on a lead. I worked like a slave to rear and train her and we nursed her and brought her through virulent distemper, with Chéron, that great Paris vet, in attendance. As soon as she realized she was seriously ill she accepted all treatments with self-possessed philosophy and I never knew a dog with such a determination to live. She was as clever as sin and as stubborn as hell. She loved no one but herself and she loved herself consumedly. When she was convalescent I would carry her about the room with only her shrewish little black face emerging from the blanket. She quite obviously

87

shared our triumph when she was pronounced out of danger and I feel sure she was confident that she would have her own way for the rest of a long life.

Very soon after her recovery she died in ten minutes of quite another ailment . . . we could have better spared a better dog. . . .

During our earlier visits we actually did some conventional sight-seeing in Paris: Versailles and the Trianon, the Malmaison, the Coinciergerie, Fontainebleau and, only once I think, we went to the Louvre. But that, I remember, was in mid-winter and the French had decided not to heat it, so we came away quickly and only lingered near the exit where they were selling small bronzes cast direct from the Egyptian originals. John gave me one of a limited edition of the little head of Akhnaton's daughter. She is very lovely on her base of Siena marble. I bought for John an exquisite Egyptian cat, elegant and sinister in the extreme. So sinister indeed that we decided he was unlucky to us and handed him on to someone less superstitious.

Once on our way back from Bagnoles de l'Orne, we visited Lisieux. It was before the building of the new Basilica and the tinted and clothed marble effigy of Thérèse still lay in the chapel of the Carmel with the Holy Father's Golden Rose in her hand. But already it was one of the greatest pilgrimages in France, masses were said daily at a dozen altars, from five in the morning until noon or later, and pilgrims came from all over the world to pay homage to the Alençon jeweller's daughter who had been so certain of the road to heaven. Blatant vulgarity was already enthroned and at High Mass when the bell rang for the Elevation, electric lights surrounding the tinted marble altarpiece spelt out: '*Je ferai tomber une pluie de roses*'. French bourgeois taste was rampant and blatant, but as Henri

Ghéon has since pointed out it is well to remember that Thérèse Martin, before she was a saint, was herself a French bourgeoise and that many of her 'clients' are of her own country and station. She is not reserved for the faithful of impeccable taste, as is testified by the curtains that flank or used to flank her shrine, entirely composed of ribbons of the Croix de Guerre, left there as tribute by soldiers who believed that they owed their lives to her protection.

And once more the café complet appears on the scene. We stayed at the rather primitive but nice little Hotel du Nord and were woken betimes by the Angelus bells. Returning to the hotel after early mass we found breakfast awaiting us in a ground-floor coffee-room. Butter and sugar were on the tables but one took one's choice from a mountain of fresh croissants piled in a corner and the cups were filled from two gigantic urns with taps that spouted forth boiling milk and coffee. . . . No wonder that one always goes back to France and forgives her deeply ingrained inhospitality.

Beauvais we visited on another occasion and Chartres, but personally I preferred Beavais. And there we loved best not the cathedral but the church of St. Eustache (or is it Etienne), that has the lovely and unforgettable windows. We stood entranced before the Tree of Jesse with its human flowers against a sapphire sky and the Lily of Salvation above them all. Later a scholarly French priest pointed out to us the deliberate vandalism that had wrecked the lower lights in the Revolution. There is another fine window in which St. Eustache kneels before a white stag with Christ between its antlers, so I expect the church is dedicated to St. Eustache and that St. Etienne is a slip of my memory. No café complet emerges from Beauvais but an excellent luncheon at a very good hotel, washed down by a memorable Mersault Charmes.

I do not think that either of us was exceptionally greedy, but it is surprising when one comes to the evoking of past happiness how often it is associated with memories of food and drink. One could never forget the flowers in Florence, the glory of them heaped round the Porcellino, but neither do I forget the *mascherpone* eaten with lashings of peach jam, nor the great blue-green Tuscan asparagus. And in memories of Fontainebleau the Château must always go hand in hand with its delectable namesake the featherweight cream cheese . . . while as for wines . . . they are memory incarnate . . . Coup de Mistral and the Côte des Maures . . . Vin Santo and Castel Toblino . . . Maddalena and Bolzano, Gewürz Traminer and Riquewihr, Castel Rametz and Merano. . . . I feel I could go on listing them indefinitely, but one of the more recent memories is among the most pleasant. A fiasco of golden sunshine bought in the station at Orvieto together with two ignoble little cardboard cups. We sat in the train face to face, John and I, with that flask between us on the little table. It was the last time we were ever to see Rome together and when we got there the flask was empty. . . . I shall not drink again of that fruit of the vine until I drink it with her . . . where she now awaits me. . . .

To return to Holland Street (a long way from Rome), it was a charming house and we lived there for four years. Something of a record for us, wandering Gentiles that we were. As a matter of fact when we decided to sell it it was not a matter of choice but of necessity, as John was in urgent need of ready money to meet the legal costs of the defence of *The Well of Loneliness*. The lease of the house was a valuable asset and it was bought on the day it was offered for sale. I remember that two applicants collided on the doorstep disputing as to which of them could claim priority.

It was, as I have said, attractive, built like a country house, with large rooms, casement windows and deep brick window-ledges where we kept bulbs and other plants. But I doubt whether in any case we should have remained in it much longer. Although we regretted it when we sold it we had, of course, already discovered that it had disadvantages. For one thing it faced uncompromisingly to the north and all the best rooms never saw the sun. Then, while there was one very large, though sunless 'best bedroom' the only other room on that floor was so small that it was barely able to accommodate a bed, so, as we had no intention of being on different floors, the only solution was for us to share a bedroom. This was convivial and in many ways we thoroughly enjoyed it, but not when John was in the throes of insomnia, when she wanted to move about or to read in bed and feared to wake me unless she lay quietly in darkness. Then there was the little baker's shop next door. It was not until the advent of summer weather that his open windows became our undoing and that shovelling and clanking echoed through the night while he stoked his fires and manipulated his ovens.

In any case, however, Holland Street had to go, and moreover it went just after John had fitted out a sunny little back room as a sitting-room for me, and back we went to Kensington Palace Mansions, but not before what seemed to be the merest chance had introduced us to Rye in Sussex.

It was just after the *Well of Loneliness* prosecutions and an acquaintance who was also a warm sympathizer asked us to come down and spend a week-end in what she called the 'little period cottage' which she had taken furnished in

Rye. I cannot now imagine what made us accept; it was not the kind of thing we were in the habit of doing, especially when invited by a comparative stranger. But accept we did and spent a week-end in what was later to be our beloved 'Forecastle', making enquiries regarding available houses. But the time was not yet ripe and we found nothing suitable though we did spend most of the following winter in Rye. The period cottage and an admirable servant were lent to John for six months by their owner, who happened to be another champion of *The Well of Loneliness*.

Whenever we could tear ourselves from police courts and lawyers we hurried down by car to the cottage, where the faithful Mabel Bourne would be there to greet us with blazing fires and her genius for cooking. It was very ugly, the little cottage in those days. Its Tudor charms were disguised almost beyond recognition by masses of heterogeneous junk and it rocked and swayed in the great souwesterly gales while Mabel hung up blankets to keep out the draughts. The bath-water was temperamental and we had only oil lamps, but to us it was a heavenly haven of peace in which we pulled ourselves together for the next round before plunging back into the battle. . . .

There was something jovial and carefree about that cottage, something that suggested 'Yo, ho, ho and a bottle of rum!' It seemed pleasantly haunted by lawless shades and its view of the Marsh was peerless. From my bed in the little room where I slept I could see the Gris Nez lighthouse on clear days and from the windows three other lighthouses flashing.

The timber ships with their tall masts and their brown sails would make their way past it along the Rother . . . but why should I attempt to write again what John has immortalized in *The Sixth Beatitude*? . . .

Later, she bought and gave me the cottage, and we christened it 'The Forecastle' and made it beautiful. So 'right' and so beautiful that everyone who saw it exclaimed with delight and admiration; we loved it very much and admired it ourselves, but in the end we looked at one another and confessed to a curious misgiving: had it become something of a museum piece? Had we somehow in destroying the vandalisms and expelling the junk also expelled something of its conviviality?

I think it was partly our experience with The Forecastle that helped us in the furnishing of our Italian apartments. In them we attempted neither style nor period but bought here and there whatever we admired and fitted it in wherever it would go. The results may have offended against highbrow canons, but were somehow very much more of a home. Moreover, since for the first time in many years we were very uncertain of our abode (we had not attempted to secure even long leases and regarded those flats at first as subsidiary to The Forecastle), we went about their furnishing with an eye to economy; we made do with many things because they were cheap, and came to the conclusion that '*le pain bênit de la gaieté*' is more often found on an unpretentious platter.

But once again I have wandered up by-ways. Before we ever owned a house in Rye we had a holiday that we never forgot; not only because it was entirely delightful and because we needed it as perhaps never before, but because by what some people call coincidence it led to the writing of *The Master of the House*.

When the prosecution of *The Well of Loneliness* had succeeded and the magistrate, having refused to hear any of our fifty-seven witnesses in its favour, had condemned it to death as an obscene book, and when the appeal (upon which

John insisted as a moral gesture though well aware that the outcome was a foregone conclusion) had for the second time condemned it to destruction, its author was not unnaturally exceedingly tired. . . .

She had, as the American journalist May Lamberton Becker expressed it, torpedoed the Ark and Mr. and Mrs. Noah had emerged and imposed their views, with temporary success, upon such territories as were under their control. What nobody foresaw was that the re-publication in Paris would be followed by translation into eleven languages, by the triumph of the book in the United States of America and the sale of more than a million copies. The author herself would probably have felt less tired had she been able to look ahead, to read in advance some of the many thousands of letters that came to her later from men and women in every walk of life, of every age and every nationality in all parts of the world, and that continued to reach her through the years and come now, even after her death, from remote places where that death is still unknown. She would have felt less tired had she known that fourteen years after publication *The Well of Loneliness* in America alone would have a steady annual sale of over one hundred thousand copies. . . . But though she was an indomitable fighter, she was no prophet, and so far as she could judge her book might well be dead. . . . There was nothing more she could do for it and she was very tired. In all her life she had never needed a rest so badly and just at that moment there came an indication that this rest might with advantage be combined with business if only she would agree to cross the Channel. . . .

Applications were being made for the rights of translation and since the book had become contraband neither manuscripts nor proofs could enter the British Isles.

Radclyffe Hall with Tulip (the dog she loved the best of all). 1931

Radclyffe Hall at Rye, Sussex. 1938.

Radclyffe Hall in 1935, a photograph by Una Troubridge.

But although there were obvious reasons for going it was some months before she would consent to go. Well aware of the notoriety that attended her wherever she went (there were many demonstrations on her behalf and many ardent champions leapt into the lists), she had a consuming fear that if she left England someone would say that her courage had failed, that she had gone abroad to let things blow over. And it was not until we had spent several months in London attending first nights and other public functions and until she had lectured for various societies that she decided that she had earned her rest and would combine it in Paris with ensuring the international survival of her book.

Paris proved pleasant but by no means restful. The story of the vicissitudes of *The Well of Loneliness* and of the victimizing of its author had preceded us; the book had been read or was being read by everyone, it was exhibited for sale in every bookshop, and since John's photograph had been in all the papers and her appearance was most individual there was no avoiding a continuous publicity.

Although John was intensely shy by nature there were aspects of this publicity that could not fail to please any author: total strangers would come up to her in the street or in a restaurant and express their admiration of the book, their amazement and indignation at its persecution. She was lionized by English, French and Americans alike and her conviction grew that the book would survive; that her labour and her stripes had not been in vain. She was sincerely grateful for the welcome and the hospitality offered by Europe and America to this exiled child of her brain. There was an abortive effort by a crank in America to imitate the exploits of James Douglas in England, but the American publishers stuck to their guns and were rewarded by a triumphant verdict in the courts, of unqualified approval and sanction.

Meanwhile, the initiator of all the trouble was getting not only tired but exhausted and not only exhausted but ill. It was plainly essential to beat a retreat and the point was to find some really quiet refuge. Colette had spoken to us of St. Tropez, where she had recently bought a property. She was wildly enthusiastic about the beauties of the Côte des Maures and raved about its bathing amenities and its unsophistication. John was far past any enthusiasm but I decided that we would make for St. Tropez and dragged her with me to Thomas Cook and Son.

There, I remember, we met with discouragement. Trains and civilization ended at St. Raphael, after which 'mesdames' must find their way as best they might by autobus or car. I also remember that there, in Cook's office, John made me a minor scene of desperation: I must be crazy to think of dragging her, tired to death as she was, to the ends of the earth, and of landing her somewhere in the unknown ... I think she said it was cruel of me!

But for reasons at that time unknown to myself I was unconvinced and I clung to my plan. The spring was upon us, the sea would be warm, Colette had enlarged upon wonderful sea bathing, upon blessed sunshine, upon nightingales and cingalas. On our way back to the hotel I conceived a plan whereby we could make the entire journey in a car which we had been hiring from the *Transports Automobiles*. It involved some juggling of mileage and charges before I could dish it up as a positive economy; obviously cheaper than travelling by train. I have always been rather an adept at this type of arithmetic. Be it as it may, John was very tired and John was always indulgent to me. John was moreover full of the idea that I had suffered strain and stress as her lieutenant in the battle and that I also badly needed a holiday. To cut a long story short, on a beautiful April morning – or was it May – we set out together in the car for St. Tropez, with Pierre the chauffeur driving, and our English maid beside him and John and I in the back of the car with Tulip, her beloved Brabançonne, and plenty of impedimenta, for the leisurely and lovely journey to the south, punctuated by the best meals that can be eaten in France. Saulieu, Mâcon, Arles, Avignon, Aix-en-Provence. We stopped for the night as we felt inclined and allowed the ex-chefs of royalty to feed us, and as the weather grew warmer we expanded, our tired nerves relaxed and we were very happy.

Before the war there were of course many thousands of rich people who did this journey frequently as a matter of course, tearing along the roads in Rolls Royces and Hispanos and Isottas, never troubling to look about them or to think about beauty, bent exclusively on 'getting there' and on making a speed record. Filling themselves at intervals with good food and drink on their way to Nice or Cannes, to Juan les Pins, and above all to the Tables at Monte Carlo. Probably they felt they had their reward and would have been patronizingly amused at us in our rather ancient hired car, with the dog and the maid and the suitcases full of books. Pottering along at a relative snail's pace (both of us cordially detested speeding), turning aside for Nîmes, Orange and the Pont du Gard, wandering through that lovely town of Arles and drinking iced Jeanne d'Arc beer at the Jules César, quite convinced that we were having the time of our lives and happily determined to make the very best of it and to enjoy every moment to the full. There were vicissitudes, of course, but in our beatific frame of mind they were taken in our stride. Despite grave warnings the English maid allowed herself to be 'treated' when we reached the wine country. I think it was at Mâcon that, when the time came to move on, she tottered into our room with a scarlet face and became strangely hilarious over the packing and over her own failure to stuff a left foot tree into one of John's right shoes . . . she was duly admonished and we resumed our journey. (I am, however, bound to admit that there came a time later on when her potations became habitual and she had to be shipped back to England.)

To me, whose only previous experience of the south of France had been that disastrous visit to Monte Carlo, every mile was a joy and a revelation. One high-light I remember was stopping the car near a little open space where the ground was thickly carpeted with low shrubs. I sniffed rapturously in the sunshine at a most unusual scent and said to John: 'What is this heavenly smell?' I was meeting the *maquis* for the first time in my life. On our way to Avignon there was another pleasant incident. The day was tropical and we were terribly hot and thirsty, beginning to wilt and to long for the next stop, when we drove through the village of Châteauneuf du Pape and right through the middle of their cherry market. Cherries were everywhere in gigantic baskets, hundreds and thousands of kilos of ripe cherries and we clamoured to Pierre to go at once and buy some. He came back with a crestfallen face to say that the sale was only '*en gros*' . . . but it took more than that to discourage us and when he had ascertained that the minimum sale was ten kilos we had them poured into the bottom of the car and ate them steadily all the way to Avignon, throwing the stones and stalks into the road . . . we sat with our feet submerged in cherries. . . .

Avignon did not come up to expectations. The Dominion

Hotel was stuffy and the food indifferent; the Brïdge was disappointingly incomplete and the heat was such that we made no attempt to visit the Papal Palace, contenting ourselves with gazing at its beautiful exterior. Arles on the other hand we simply adored. We drank much iced beer in a loggia at the Jules César and walked the colourful streets until late at night. But the best of all that wonderful journey, in which every joy was doubled by being shared, and in which John's pleasure was I think more than doubled because she was showman to my inexperience, was waking in the morning at the Napoléon at St. Raphael with the southern sky as blue as a sapphire, the warm air pouring in at the wide-open windows together with the multiple sounds of a harbour. . . . And on going to the window the blue Mediterranean and the ships and boats of all shapes and sizes with their brilliant hulls and red or tawny sails. . . . To see it all for the first time is truly an unforgettable experience. I also met on that morning, walking on my pyjamas, an unknown and unpleasant-looking insect that was to become only too familiar: the tick that is known as the '*poux des bois*', and that was to become the bane of poor little Tulip's life. We had not known that throughout the south of France this voracious little horror is ubiquitous and that one of our daily duties throughout our stay would be going over the unhappy little beast every evening and carefully removing these pests intact!

A temporary set-back met us on arrival at St. Tropez. Colette had warmly recommended a pension kept by an English couple. When we arrived there we were momentarily dismayed. The rooms were unfriendly and gloomy, under heavy over-hanging eaves. Food must compulsorily be eaten out of doors with a total disregard of the antics of the mistral. Moreover the house stood in such a position that bathing necessitated a considerable walk down and up something very like a precipice. Added to all this, not only the proprietors but the entire outfit was aggressively English, and we had not travelled half across Europe to build South Kensington in France's green and pleasant land. . . . It happened to be a relatively chilly day and we ate an inferior and tepid meal in a draughty garden. It was served to us by people who obviously reciprocated our distaste. But we held a quiet council of war: Pierre and the car were requisitioned after luncheon and by that evening we were settled in beautiful rooms, with balconies overlooking the private bathing beach, at the Golf Hotel, Beauvallon. There we were to remain for several happy months.

But it was just at the final stage of our enchanted pilgrimage that there occurred an incident which made me wonder whether, just possibly, in my stubborn determination to come to St. Tropez, I had been influenced by forces of which I was unconscious.

Many months before we undertook this journey John had said to me that she was haunted by the desire to write a book about a boy of our own times, the son of a carpenter, who, as he grew up in the carpenter's shop, would have memories and impulses that he did not understand, that linked him with the Carpenter's Son of Nazareth.

But she had added that she was unable to begin the book as she could not visualize its geographical setting . . . she had no conception of the place or country in which her hero would come to birth. She had not, so far as I was concerned, mentioned this idea on more than one occasion. I was actually unaware that she was dwelling upon it: she was often silent when 'hatching' a book. In fact there were times when she was so silent that she would take the trouble to reassure me and would say: 'If I'm silent, it isn't bad temper, darling, it's just that I'm "broody" over my work'. . . .

But on this occasion the unwritten book was lying barely under the surface, and as our car made its way through Fréjus she suddenly grasped my arm and called to Pierre to stop. What had caught her eye was a low stone archway and under the archway, half in and half out of it, a carpenter's bench and a carpenter at work. 'Look,' she said, 'there is my carpenter's shop. That's where Christophe Bénédit was born. . . .'

And so the holiday undertaken for our pleasure became also the perfect occasion she needed for collecting copy detail for her book. In Provence we remained till her reservoir was filled, and to make matters easier, the Parisian Pierre, who had long since replaced his 'casquette' by a bérèt, turned out to be himself a native of Provence, speaking the language, knowing the country and even adept at the local talent of catching a cingala unharmed in his hand so that we were able to examine it at leisure.

All of which does not mean that we gave up our holiday or that John made the slightest attempt to work. We had come to Beauvallon to rest and rest we did, and in any case John seldom worked when she was collecting material. Some people would have called our resting rather strenuous. Its main feature was to wear as few clothes as possible and to bathe, and to bathe and to bathe, three or more times a day and for increasingly long periods and in this excess John was the principal sinner. If ever I lost sight of her on the beach for a moment and inquired her whereabouts the answer was invariably: '*Elle est dans la mer.* . . .' She grew as brown as a berry and her hair got bleached and her eyes were clear and very blue and her teeth very white in her tanned face. . . . All the lines of strain and anxiety seemed to disappear and her smile grew rakish and carefree again and I think I never knew her to be so well. I myself had grown positively stout: I turned the scales at nearly eight stone and was mahogany coloured all over. . . . Oh yes, it was indeed a holiday of holidays, and a snapshot has remained to bear testimony to it. It is of myself bare-legged, bare-footed and hatless, looking black in a low-necked sleeveless jumper and of John in ragged linen slacks and a ragamuffin hat sitting on the beach beside me, grinning. . . .

We would spend whole days sometimes over at St. Tropez and evenings at the then unspoiled Café de l'Escale, and I remember a crazy midday climb up to the Citadel. . . . I suspect John of having tried to discover for herself the exact sensations of Christophe Bénédit when he climbed to the Citadel with Jan. Once again, I feel, why should I try to describe what she has written for ever? But at any rate no one in *The Master of the House* bathed in a state of nature at Les Salins, lay in the shallow pools among the hot seaweed and ate lobsters afterwards at the admirable restaurant that was temporarily established on the beach. I remember our delight in finding that the beach in question was entirely composed of tiny shells and corals; the sea was a lucent jade-green. With the coming of June the *maquis* lost its scent but the nightingales sang even at midday.

We also went often to Ste. Maxime and St. Raphael and to all the little ports along the coast: Ste. Croix, Le Lavandou and St. Peire and at least a dozen others we visited and explored. In fact St. Loup-sur-Mer was something of a composite, though primarily, of course, drawn from St. Tropez: the characters of the book were purely imaginary, with possibly one exception. And here I must make a statement that will inevitably involve a lengthy digression.

Quite unconsciously Radclyffe Hall wrote herself into the character of Christophe Bénédit. She neither acknowledged nor realized the fact, but I who knew her better than anyone on this earth affirm it.

Moreover, although it is true that always, while she created her characters, they came alive to her to an extraordinary degree, so much so that at times she would awake from sleep to find herself actually talking to them. While it is also true that in *The Well of Loneliness* many of Stephen Gordon's feelings and reactions, though practically none of her circumstances or experiences, were her own . . . (had she not always maintained that only by an invert could such a book be written?) it was only with Christophe Bénédit that she identified herself spiritually, mentally and physically to an extent of which she herself remained always completely unconscious.

She undertook the writing of *The Master of the House* with conscious solemnity of purpose and her life while at work upon it was deliberately austere.

While she was engaged upon it she derived great happiness from an unexpected occurrence which struck us both as excluding coincidence.

A dear friend and neighbour from Smallhythe, Tony Atwood, suddenly asked us if we would take charge of a Relic of True Cross which was in her possession and if possible give it the reverent exposition in our house that her circumstances at that time precluded her from doing.

The Relic was duly placed with the obligatory light in a shrine in my bedroom and remained there throughout the writing of a book of which a reader (not a Catholic but a Unitarian minister) wrote from America to the publishers: 'There is an unearthly radiance hovering over the book . . . It is almost like reading the gospels.'

The Master of the House was in any case the product of a profound and painful spiritual reaction.

At the time of James Douglas's attack upon *The Well of Loneliness,* together with many splendid evidences of sympathy, admiration and respect, there had been published a peculiarly vile, obscene and blasphemous caricature of the author which had not only disgusted and horrified us both but which had caused her such deep spiritual pain that throughout the remaining years of her life she could scarcely bear to speak of it, even to me. Once she did say: 'To think that I should have been used as a means of disrespect to Him . . .', nor did her complete helplessness and innocence in the matter seem to afford her any consolation.

The Master of the House was written as an amends for that insult to her Lord and to her Faith, and as such that book was nearer and dearer to her heart than anything she wrote before it or afterwards.

In it, and with Christophe Bénédit, she believed, pitied, loved and suffered, and as she approached the writing of his martyrdom she became more and more absorbed in an intensive study of the Passion of Christ. It was at this time that a curious incident occurred which I shall merely set down without any attempt at explanation.

She began to complain to me of continual and growing discomfort in the palm of her right hand which interfered with her writing. Very soon the same trouble appeared also in the palm of the other hand; moreover the discomfort increased gradually to very severe pain. She described it as an intense irritation combined with sharp stabbing pain. It prevented her sleeping, gave her no peace and effectually defeated even her very vital inspirational concentration. We repeatedly and minutely examined the palms of her hands, finding no visible lesion of any kind, but as she suggested that it might be some kind of invisible eczema we applied a succession of salves and lotions with less than no result.

The pain increased and soon she sat with both hands bandaged, trying vainly to concentrate and deeply resentful of this interference with her work.

It was only when we noticed that an angry-looking red stain was appearing in the centre of both palms that we decided it was time to consult a doctor and it was he who, after having unsuccessfully prescribed various applications and even medicines, recommended treatment by deep rays.

By this time the marks on both palms were clearly defined. In one hand the red stain was an oval about half an inch wide by three quarters of an inch in length. In the other hand, the right one, it was slightly larger and extended in a line as though some liquid had been poured into the palm and had run towards the wrist, leaving a trail of inflamation.

One very brief treatment by an eminent radiologist was followed almost immediately, and for several hours, by such unendurable agony that I was distracted and rang him up to know whether he had used an unusually severe application. He asked me to come round at once and assured me that the contrary was the case; that he had been particularly careful to begin with the mildest treatment possible and was quite unable to account for her condition.

After that experience we had no further recourse to remedies; she endured as best she might and very gradually the pain diminished and the stains faded . . . it was not until they had disappeared that it struck me that they might have had a connexion with the subject of the work upon which she was engaged. . . .

And so, after this disgression, back to Beauvallon where that memorable holiday was coming to an end, and presently we were back in England and almost immediately after that we were back in Rye. Having as yet no home, we went to the 'Mermaid' and were perfectly happy there in antique discomfort. It was then in an extreme state of neglect and dilapidation. It was dirty, badly heated and when fires became necessary, the chimneys smoked. The ancient windows let in arctic draughts and we were reduced to stuffing cracks and holes with stockings. But we camped in a large and beautiful room with a big log fire in a lovely old grate, and we tolerated a stinking supplementary oilstove and a host of other inconveniences with equanimity, and John was able to work because of the fulfilling atmosphere of the place. We also liked the inefficient old Irish manageress. Our attitude can best be gauged by John's reactions when we lunched one day at another and at that time decidedly better equipped hotel. She was told that in deference to certain old maids of both sexes it was not permitted to smoke in the coffee-room and she remarked very audibly to me: 'Let's go back to our Mermaid, shall we? At any rate there I'm allowed to spit on the floor!'

We did not at first succeed in our hunt for a home; she was going to give me the house when we found it and was very anxious this time to make no mistakes. It had to be not only convenient but beautiful and not only beautiful but also ancient and unspoiled, and houses of that description are seldom empty in Rye.

Meanwhile, in spite of our love for the Mermaid, we felt we must have more room to spread ourselves and we compromised by taking a little furnished house, No. 8 Watchbell Street, exactly opposite the Catholic church. There she could work quietly and keep her own hours and meanwhile we would have time to look around us at leisure until we should find what we really wanted. No. 8 was rather a pleasant little house; quite modern and with no pretensions to beauty, but it had one feature that we dearly loved. From its sitting-room, when the church door was open, we could look right through it up the nave and see the statue of the Sacred Heart softly illumined in the darkness by the votive candles that burned before it.

We secured the services of the admirable Mabel Bourne, who had already worked for us at the cottage and who followed our fortunes for seven years, and we went on looking at every house that became available until at last we found something which we felt to be worth while.

Of course we had aimed at perfection and did not find it; from the first we knew that the house had obvious defects. For one thing its situation was a drawback: in the High Street plumb in the middle of all the shops. But it nevertheless had features that delighted us. It was one of the oldest houses in the town and had once been part of the monastery of Friars Heremite of St. Augustine. It was said to date from the Fourteenth century and such parts of it as had already been restored to their original condition disclosed timbers, in some instances, seventeen inches across. Most of it had been vandalized in the time of Good Queen Anne but our predecessors had begun the stripping and had revealed enough to arouse our enthusiasm and our expectations. There was a long room with huge rafters and a fine open grate which would be an ideal study for John, and stripping had already uncovered a pre-Tudor fresco in the bedroom that was to be mine. John bought the house for me, we christened it 'The Black Boy', arrayed ourselves in boiler suits and there followed glorious weeks of discovery. We hacked with fireaxes and even with pickaxes, we pulled down ceilings upon our heads, we tore down walls and uncovered bricks, finding in the process a priest's hiding hole and a beautiful Henry VII fireplace. We also found a silver groat of Henry VIII and other relics almost as interesting. We had an exhausting but entrancing orgy, and since appetite grows with eating we were later to repeat the process with two other ancient Rye houses.

When we had done our best, or our worst, with 'The Black Boy' we settled in to a very comfortable home. We admired it ourselves and so did other people and we did not mind the fact that it was unmistakably haunted. We were both quite certain that we liked the haunt and that it liked us, and as a matter of fact we were both equally and simultaneously certain that when we had lived in the house for a couple of years our haunt quite suddenly and unmistakably left us and left the house blankly devoid of all atmosphere. . . . I think we regretted our mysterious familiar. . . .

In any case, by the time it departed various things had happened indicating that our days at 'The Black Boy' were drawing to a close.

One of the first signs of a new order came in the fact that after a time John had decided that unadulterated Rye was not sufficiently stimulating to her brain; that she needed the contacts of life in a city to an extent not supplied by visits to a London hotel. So we took a tiny flat on a fifth floor in St. Martin's Lane and knew yet again the raptures of home-making!

I think it is only fair to John to say that when we gave up that flat after about a year, it was my heart and not her fickle fancy that was responsible, or perhaps the fickle fancy of the lift! After eleven o'clock at night, or on such occasion as it went on strike, there was nothing for it but to toil up the five flights and this exercise began to affect me rather unpleasantly.

But, for that matter, the flat outlived 'The Black Boy'. John had lost money in the American slump and her income had thereby been practically halved. Our personal maid (of the 'useful' type) had to go and if we were to retain the London flat we must look out for humbler quarters in Rye . . . something that would involve less upkeep and less staff. It was just at that moment that the cottage in the Hucksteps, in which we had passed our first night in Rye, became available at a very low figure. We sold 'The Black Boy' and she gave me 'The Forecastle' which, little as we knew it, was to be our last home in England.

Altogether we lived in Rye for a good many years, off and on; lived there, I mean, in the sense that it was our home to which we returned: from London, from Paris, from Bagnoles, from Italy. We dearly loved the cottage and the little town with its arrogant motto: 'God save Englonde and the Towne of Rye', and I think John has made her love of it very obvious in *The Sixth Beatitude*. Even after years of familiarity it kept its glamour; we collected every book that mentioned it and John paid absurd prices in order to give me a Daniel Gill clock, Holloway's *History of Rye* and Jeake's *Charters of the Cinque Ports*.

I remember one of the last Christmases we spent there. We had left a convivial party late on Christmas eve and had come out into brilliant frosty moonlight. We could not make up our minds to go home and walked about staring at the moonlit streets until past three o'clock in the morning.

We also loved the marsh, and Smallhythe, a few miles away, where lived our friends Edy Craig, Christopher St. John and Tony Atwood in what must be one of the loveliest cottages upon earth with its garden that merges into the marsh.

If either of us had been ill or unwell, we always resumed life with one particular drive: along to Appledore by the side of the Military Canal, to Tenterden and then home again through Smallhythe . . . we used to think and say that we could never leave Rye.

And yet during the last nine years of John's life I do not think we were more than one year in England, and when we returned in 1939, it was to sell 'The Forecastle' with the intention of living out the rest of our days in Italy.

It was while we were at 'The Black Boy' that John lost Tulip, the little Brabançonne who had gone south with us. She had been brought to Paris from Brussels for our inspection and with both John and the dog it had been love at first sight. She was not tiny, but quite small and very beautiful. The colour of mahogany, with cropped ears, huge eyes, a perfect head and an expression that was all her own. Her adoration of John was such that she treated even me as a stranger and refused to go with me for even necessary outings. But her love was not selfish and she would lie in her basket happily for hours while John sat working, perfectly satisfied in the presence of her God and with an occasional word of affection. She seemed quite robust but she evidently lacked stamina; actually she was unpardonably inbred and had six toes on each of her little round feet. When illness came it was quickly over. She was buried in the garden with a small square tombstone which went with us later when we moved to 'The Forecastle'. John mourned her deeply and never forgot her; in fact it was several years before she would consent to have another dog of her own, and it was not until we were settled in Florence that she bought a dog in the street as a rescue and came to love him almost as dearly as Tulip. That dog was Fido, her big white poodle. He survived her, as did another rescue, Jane, a comely King Charles spaniel which she bought from a bombed area during the Battle of Britain.

I am perfectly aware that for people who do not love dogs, there will be too much about them in this story of John's life; but it is her life I am writing and not theirs, and to her, from childhood onwards, dogs were always an integral part of existence.

On that last terrible journey by ambulance to London she insisted upon stopping the ambulance at Taunton so that the two dogs should be personally handed over to the vet who would take care of them, and only a few weeks before her death, she herself gave me instructions as to their future . . . she was quite convinced that she would meet them again together with all the animals she had loved.

It was while we were living at 'The Black Boy' in the summer of 1932 that I became suddenly and seriously ill, was taken to London for a major operation, and three days later very nearly left John and this earth. The operation had been perfectly successful but my heart had always been a doubtful quantity and nearly went back on us altogether. I sometimes feel that I must have been much more selfish than I had ever admitted to myself, because when I look back upon that grave and at first painful illness, which to John was always a nightmare memory, all I can remember is perfect happiness. Physical pain and discomfort are so easily forgotten, but not the ceaseless and loving care that made them not only endurable but of little consequence . . . The warm, happy consciousness of being absolutely essential to the one being on earth who is all in all.

Very clear memories have remained of that illness: one of weakness and weariness beyond belief that refused all nourishment and was only asking to slip away out of life, and of suddenly opening my eyes and seeing John sitting beside me with her head in her hands in an attitude of complete and utter despair . . . I could not leave her and I dragged myself back to life and thereafter accepted what I was offered. . . . Of the peaches that multiplied as though by magic because I had once accepted a peach . . . of the flowers that also became more beautiful and more plentiful when the length of my illness had gradually led to a dearth of offerings from the outside world . . . of my conspiring with the nurse a little later to let me make up skilfully so that when John came to me in the morning she was cheered by a faint colour in my lips and cheeks . . . I remember also that she was suspicious and questioned me and that I lied to her for perhaps the only time in my life. But by then I was beginning to notice the ravages that my illness had wrought in her face . . . And I must be less selfish now than I was in those days for, now that I am left alone, I thank God humbly that she did not survive me and that I have been the one to suffer bereavement.

The day came when I left the nursing home and she bore me off in triumph to Brighton, where she pushed me for miles along the sea front in a wheeled chair until I gradually recovered my strength. And so, back to Rye and to eleven more years, during which I used often secretly to calculate how many years of life together we might hope for before the coming of old age and death. Always there was a lurking fear of separation and less confidence than I now have in ultimate reunion.

I have written very little here about our friends and this I think for the following reason: although we had of course many good friends and acquaintances, both in England and abroad, who through circumstances or proximity moved in or out of our intimacy, the very fact of our perfect companionship precluded their assuming any great importance or entering very closely into our lives. But some do stand out, for one reason or another, as I look back through the years.

There was Ida Temple, a jovial Irishwoman who had married an Englishman above her in station but greatly her inferior in heart and generosity. Not long after we met her she was left a widow with three growing children and for quite six years we always spent Christmas at her comfortable Victorian house in Datchet. We felt that something we really valued had gone when she died suddenly. There was Toupie Lowther, who had known and admired Ladye and who used to visit us at Chip Chase. A strange creature she was, a remarkable athlete who did fine work in the First World War. But she was essentially a crank. A compound of the very male and very feminine. She passed out of our lives when John wrote *The Well of Loneliness,* and we afterwards heard that she had resented the book as challenging her claim to be the only invert in existence. Later still, when she was growing very old, I was told that she had moreover acquired the illusion that she had served as a model for Stephen Gordon! She also is dead now, peace be upon her . . . and doubtless has shed her illusions. At Smallhythe, as I have said before, were Edy Craig, Christopher St. John, Tony Atwood, and Olive Chaplin, and many happy hours were spent with them, and we all shared many light-hearted convivial meals, there and in their London flat. Dodo Benson was also a neighbour, in Rye, and so for a time was Francis Yeats-Brown, and latterly there was Naomi Jacob at Sirmione. But any attempt to evoke such memories quickly degenerates into a mere list of names, to which could be added so many others in America, in France and particularly in Italy; friends of whom we were genuinely fond, but nevertheless we were always sufficient unto ourselves, and I think people insensibly felt it.

It was not until the summer of 1934 that a third person entered more intimately into our lives and the consequences for a number of years were not happy for either of us or for her.

In the spring of that year, having prepared 'The Forecastle' for our own occupation and being greatly delighted with the results, we almost decided to move in at once and settle down there for the summer. John was anxious to get back to her work, which had been somewhat interrupted by the vicissitudes of moving house. But she was far from well and moreover her old enemy the 'hunting vein' was giving her trouble and I put great pressure on her to postpone her return to work and to make up her mind to do a cure again at Bagnoles de l'Orne. I always remember how earnestly she opposed me and how I overbore her protests in my anxiety for the good of her health. She told me afterwards, many times, that she had had an almost overwhelming instinct against leaving England on that occasion and had been unable to understand her own forebodings.

In the end, however, she gave in to me, I made all arrangements and on a very hot day in June we crossed the Channel in a flat calm and found ourselves once more in Paris. We were there a couple of days and it proved a most delightful visit. Colette, Romaine Brooks, Natalie Barney and Madame de Clermont Tonnerre, all good friends who always seemed as glad to see us as we were glad to find them again, vied with each other to entertain us and when we boarded the train for Bagnoles we agreed that we had enjoyed every moment of our stay.

But the weather had been torrid and moreover thundery

and somehow I had been poisoned or had acquired a germ (our dear Dr. Joly, who was hastily summoned, attributed the trouble to drinking iced water when over-heated) and no sooner did we reach our destination than I went down with a violent attack of enteritis. So, far from being able to rest and take the baths, John found herself nursing me night and day while my temperature climbed steadily up the thermometer and I was soon too weak to stir from my bed. Moreover the doctor proved completely helpless in the urgent matter of providing a nurse. However, being still in full possession of my senses, I decided that John had not come to Bagnoles to wear herself out and I telephoned to the American Hospital of Paris and asked them to send us a nurse immediately. This they did and on the following day Evguenia Souline arrived to nurse me.

Incidentally she was a devoted and admirable nurse and I was never better taken care of in my life, but it never for one moment entered my mind that this young Russian woman with the curious face – the refugee daughter of a deceased Tzarist Cossack general – was to be anything in our lives but a bird of passage. At most I contemplated the possibility of inviting her to a meal when we returned to Paris and taking her to the Opera or to a theatre. But the utterly unexpected does happen, and she was destined to become a very intimate part of our daily existance for the remaining nine years of John's life.

It was not to be a happy connexion for either John or Evguenia; John was a sensitive, highly-evolved European, utterly incapable of divorcing any emotional impulse from all that was protective and kind in her nature. Even apart from her devotion to me, she always offered good coin in genuine affection.

Evguenia was a creature of impulses and violent surface

emotions; she was indeed as violent and uncontrolled as a savage, and while she undoubtedly at first gave John such affection as it lay in her nature to give, she had little or no use for tenderness or protection, which she easily mistook for tyranny and interference. Intelligent as she was and capable in many ways, with a genuine appreciation of art and music, John's work was to her a matter of no interest and could only, in her view, be a very subsidiary consideration, and indeed a matter for resentment.

Both John and I knew that she felt it to be an interference with the agreeable aspects of life as she wished to live it. She did not like to feel herself overshadowed by John's established literary eminence.

She had less than no appreciation of the conditions essential to the production of creative work and was intensely bored whenever John was immersed in it. I have reason to believe that even after a number of years Evguenia hardly knew the names of the characters that John had created.

Almost from the first she and John were oil and water and their relationship, after a very brief spell of relative peacefulness, became chiefly an affair of storms and reconciliations. Nor was the situation improved when only a few months after we came to know her Evguenia was smitten down with what appeared to be a recurrence of the lung trouble from which she had suffered on two previous occasions.

In John all that was finest came at once to the surface; all her genius for compassion and protection was concentrated upon a determination to restore this afflicted friend to health. I can look back upon her patience, her endurance, her complete selflessness with immense pride and I am thankful to remember that in spite of my inevitable jealousy, and my distress at such a disastrous interruption to her work,

I rallied whole-heartedly to her determination that we should devote our combined energies to that end.

On the advice of the Paris doctor, as soon as Evguenia was fit to travel we took her to Grasse where she was to remain until the summer, submitting herself to a modified form of treatment. From the first to the last she was an impossible patient, as difficult to control as a bucking bronco, headstrong and wild and inconsistent, with alternating moods of incoherent rage, of abysmal gloom and crazy optimism, and from first to last John bore with them all, realizing always the element of childishness that was a racial component of this Cossack nature.

Dr. Berthier, who attended Evguenia in Grasse, pronounced her to be sound at the end of four months, but he told us that if her health was to be maintained on secure foundations, three winters in succession should be spent in the south, and that London or Paris winters should be permanently avoided, and this verdict it was that led to our remaining abroad and only occasionally visiting Rye in the summer. We took Evguenia to Merano for the winter of 1936 and the following years were spent in Florence.

And there I shall leave discussion of this situation. To a degree that lessened as the years passed, Evguenia remained with us wherever we went, either staying with us in hotels or occupying quarters of her own near-by. This was in accordance with my wishes which John consulted as she did in all things, and I still think that while it had its disadvantages it was in the long run the best solution. John's health was already very far from robust and Evguenia in spite of her nursing experience had no conception of how to take care of her. Moreover, except very rarely for a few days, John hated leaving me and was always anxious when away from me. Latterly Evguenia at her own wish largely went her own way and John thought it better to allow her to do so, while always seeing that she wanted for nothing, and, whether she felt the need of them or not, was consistently the object of solicitude and affection. That solicitude and a measure of the affection were continued until the day of John's death.

But, as I have already said, our meeting with Evguenia was not in the first instance allowed to alter our plans and when she returned to Paris we went on to Sirmione to rooms engaged for us by Mickie Jacob who hitherto an acquaintance only by correspondence, soon became, and has remained, a very dear personal friend. And while we were there an event took place which even in the midst of distress and anxiety gave John as well as myself considerable pleasure.

For many years, previous indeed to my meeting John, and as soon as I had become familiar with the Italian language, I had deeply admired all the works of the poet-patriot, Gabriele d'Annunzio, and had long wished to meet him in person.

On reaching Sirmione I perceived for the first time a possible opportunity of gratifying that wish. The Vittoriale, d'Annunzio's palatial villa, was only a few miles from Sirmione and as John's books had been translated into Italian and had earned her a very considerable literary reputation in Italy, it seemed perfectly permissible that while staying in the neighbourhood she should send him a copy of the Italian translation of *The Well of Loneliness* and ask whether she might be permitted, accompanied by her friend Lady Troubridge, to pay her respects to the great Italian writer. This procedure had been recommended to me by Romaine Brooks (who had known him well for many years) as the only one likely to penetrate his determined seclusion. She had said that personal introductions were useless and that the only valid passport to his demesne was literary eminence and reputation.

I put the matter up to John and was met by a blank and horrified refusal: she was shy; she had never done such a thing in her life; moreover her Italian, though by this time fluent, was entirely unorthodox, and in the unlikely event of his agreeing to receive us she would be tongue-tied with embarrassment and certain to make a complete fool of herself.

But dropping will wear a stone and I was very reluctant to lose an opportunity that might never recur. I pointed out that without her I could do nothing and that I had seldom seriously asked her to oblige me by doing violence to her shyness. I bought the requisite copy of *Il Pozzo della Solitudine* in Verona, I drafted a suitable letter designed to save her trouble and finally she yielded to my importunity.

She wrote a letter of her own and posted it together with the book and begged me not to build up hopes that were bound to be disappointed, as it was well known throughout the neighbourhood that 'Il Comandante' (the only title by which he consented to be known) had for a long time past been a complete recluse and refused to receive even his old comrades in arms. Many had been the efforts made to gain admittance to the magnificent palace that was also his prison . . . (the carabinieri at the gates and the salute fired whenever he left or returned to his home were quite as much a government precaution as a tribute of respect). Throughout Italy, after his fantastic exploits in the air, on land and sea during the First World War . . . (it should be remembered that it was his speech at Quarto that brought Italy into it as our ally . . .) and particularly since the adventure of Fiume, his name had become one with which to conjure and his slightest movement a matter for universal interest.

Ten days went by after we had posted the letter, and I had begun to believe that John had been right, when very suddenly the oracle spoke. At that time there was only one telephone in Sirmione, a public box attached to the post office, which delivered messages throughout the promontory, its officials having thus every opportunity of learning and broadcasting their nature. It was in a breathless state of excitement that Annita, the little hotel waitress, came running to us on the evening of the eleventh day gasping that there was a message from the Vittoriale. The folded paper she held informed Radclyffe Hall that on the following day a car might be expected which would bring her a letter from the Comandante. By this time John also was getting excited, and the excitement grew when at noon the next day a further telephone message was delivered to the effect that the car had now left the Vittoriale. It was therefore due to arrive at any minute and all Sirmione was out to watch for it, with the exception, however, of John herself who, having been viciously stung by a horse-fly, was nursing a swollen ankle in our bedroom. Personally I was hanging out of the window when at last the car arrived at the door: a racing Alfa Romeo with a little pennant sporting the colours of the Prince of Monte Nevoso. Of course I was down the stairs in a moment, in time to greet an elderly lady, carrying a folio envelope covered with blue seals, addressed in a large and ornamental script to 'Radclyffe Hall al'Albergo Catullo'. This, moreover, she refused to part with, having received orders to deliver it directly into John's hands.

I explained that John was unable to come downstairs so a procession set out up the stairs to find her. Mademoiselle Aélis grasping the letter and also some additional and more bulky envelopes, the hotel porter bearing a huge bouquet of carnations surrounded by laurels and tied with the blue and red ribbon of Monte Nevoso, and finally Annita clasping a large bowl which later proved to be of special procelain embodying the Comandante's 'Device of the Cornucopia' with his motto : '*Io ho quel che ho donato*'. It was full of golden muscat grapes, gathered, as he told her in the letter, 'in his secret orchard' and sprinkled with the petals of yellow roses. The bowl was wrapped in a large blue and red silk hankerchief woven with another of d'Annunzio's devices.

The bulky envelopes contained jewellery; bracelets for us both of rubies, sapphires and platinum fashioned by Mastro Paragon Coppella, the resident goldsmith of the Vittoriale. Other valuable jewels there were, and copies of his books inscribed to John, but surpassing all else in interest, the letter. He had read, it seemed, *The Well of Loneliness,* of which he wrote with deep admiration, and all this Medicean splendour of gifts was designed to honour the writer of so fine a work. He demanded the original edition in English of which, he assured her, he had considerable knowledge; he said that he wished her to come and see him, but (and surely this was the irony of fate) that as he was now no longer a young man, he saw only such people as were his colleagues in literature and he felt sure that I would be understanding if he asked her to come and talk with him alone! 'a tre occhi' – an allusion to the fact that he himself had only the sight of one eye! Incidentally he had forgotten to fix the appointment.

John was almost as much distressed as she was pleased. She fully appreciated the honour he did her, being herself an ardent admirer of his work; but she was miserable at the thought of my disappointment! However, there was obviously nothing to be done about it, and the following

121

day the car returned in the early afternoon with Mademoiselle Aélis, commissioned to fetch her. There was also another most interesting letter, more valuable gifts for both of us and a series of photographs of the poet himself from early adolescence until the present day. It was then that the kindly Aélis suggested that as the Comandante had told her that he might agree to seeing me later, after his tête-à-tête with his fellow-author, I had better accompany them as far as Gardone and wait in the hotel in case I should be summoned. She explained that he had little sense of expediency and was quite capable at any time during the afternoon or evening of suddenly making up his mind that he wished to see me and expecting my immediate presence as though by magic. So the three of us got into the Alfa Romeo and off we went at terrific speed, driven by an ex-ace of the Comandante's squadron. The road was kept clear all the way for the car, the note of its horn being familiar to the local people. I was deposited at the Grand Hotel in Gardone and at four o'clock in the afternoon John was driven up to the Vittoriale. I shall not easily forget that afternoon and evening. I sat in the torried heat of that hotel for nearly eight hours, literally eaten alive by mosquitoes and possessing my disappointed soul in such patience as I could muster, reading the inscribed copy of the *Fiore delle Laudi* which the Comandante had sent me, presumably to keep me quiet! At about half past eight the faithful Aélis telephoned: John and the Comandante had gone in to a tête-à-tête dinner, he had spurned a timid suggestion that I might be sent for and I had better get something to eat where I was.

It was nearly midnight when the car appeared, containing John knee-deep in more gifts, a John who was grinning with sheer delight because she was the bearer of an invitation – we were both to return on the following afternoon and the Comandante, when showing her his study, had said he would not show her his manuscripts until Una came. . . .

Another headlong drive, in the dark this time, under an Italian night of stars while John poured forth the tale of the hours she had spent, enthralled by this great little one-eyed genius. I am glad to say that very soon afterwards and before there had been time for her impressions to get blunted she embodied the account of her experience in a lecture, of which the manuscript is still in existence.

But it seems that I was fated never to meet him. The next day, to John's intense amusement, as soon as we had had luncheon I prepared for the long-desired visit . . . I certainly did set out to make the best of myself, with a kind of feeling that I must do John credit . . . but there came another of those telephone messages from the Vittoriale: the Comandante deeply regretted but he was not well and would be unable to receive us that day. And on the next day we left Sirmione for Paris.

John's disappointment on my behalf far exceeded my own. She kept on saying that it had all been grossly unfair, that of the two of us I had been the more anxious to know him . . . but as usual the powers that be knew their own business, and for both of them their meeting had been more than a passing incident. He had made many plans for further meetings: she was to dedicate her next book to him and it was to be written in a villa on his estate in which we were to live indefinitely as his guests. But illness and melancholia claimed him as their victims and none of these plans was fated to materialize. Nevertheless, though they were never to see each other again on this earth, John gave him from that moment a genuine affection and he seemed to appreciate and to return it, for from time to time he would send her messages asking her to write to him as she had promised to do. He would also reserve for her special copies of his books as they were published. Unable himself to believe in immortality and a prey to a depression approaching melancholia he clung to the thought of her unwavering faith and would not allow her to go out of his life.

On two occasions he went so far as to ask her to come to him and each time she answered the summons. But when we reached Gardone and went up to the Vittoriale he gave way to his curious mental affliction that caused him to hide even from his nearest and dearest, and except that we made a very good friend of his devoted châtelaine, Luisa Bàccara, we might as well have remained away; he never again emerged from his seclusion.

Twice we spent a week at the Grand Hotel in Gardone, waiting for the summons that never came, and at intervals the car would come down from the villa to fetch the letters which he begged her to write . . . there was a curious affinity of some sort between them, in which I could never have had any part.

The second time that we made the journey we were staying at Merano in the Tyrol and we drove to Gardone in the middle of April through that incredible Adige Valley. The sky was of sapphire overhead, the immense mountain peaks wore their winter snows and we drove through miles and miles of blossoming trees shading from crimson to paper-white, and lunched by the lakeside at lovely Malcesine.

Of all the gifts the Comandante gave her she treasured most the silver medal of the British Literary Society. It had been presented to 'Gabriele d'Annunzio, poeta e voce *d'Italia*', and bitterly resenting on her behalf the persecution of *The Well of Loneliness* by her own country, he sent it to her '*honoris causa*'.

John wept for him when she heard he was dead.

Merano . . . that was where we took Evguenia the second winter after she fell ill. She had hated Grasse after a momentary admiration of its beauty, and indeed, except for such people as John and myself who, so long as we had books and each other could never know boredom, there wasn't much to do there or much variety, especially as she was debarred from long walks or excursions.

But when Evguenia was unhappy she was turbulent and so when another winter was looming ahead, after a summer spent at Trois Epis in pious Alsace, among the wayside crucifixes, the Hans Andersen villages and the storks, we cast about for somewhere to go which would combine a good climate with some measure of distraction. At first we made arrangements to go to Pau, but news of the civil war in Spain became disquieting. In those days the idea of aerial warfare on the frontier and possibly extending into our vicinity seemed as strange as it was unpleasant, especially with a semi-invalid to be considered, and racking our brains for a suitable alternative we remembered Mickie Jacob at Sirmione and her glowing account of Merano.

We arrived there, I remember, late on a November afternoon, after a chilly night spent at Verona and a cold and uncomfortable journey, and we drove from the station to the hotel through what seemed to be a particularly unattractive modern Italian town and in spite of some beautiful mountains in the distance, we began to wonder why we had come. The next day, however, when Evguenia was resting, John and I set out to explore and very soon we discovered the old Merano.

The Portici with their frescoed arches leading to the beautiful old Piazza and to the Duomo with the giant Saint Christopher painted on its outer wall. . . . The lovely Passirio river and the walk above the town, the Tappeinerweg, cumbrously re-christened by the Italians, Passeggiata Principessa di Piemonte ! We came to love Merano very much indeed, especially when it celebrated Christmas by carols sung after the midnight mass from the summit of the tower of the Duomo . . . 'Heilige Nacht' into the frozen air to an accompaniment of silver trumpets. We came to love the truculent Tyrolese with their insuperable dislike of any control, be it Austrian or Italian, and we were fascinated by their national costumes, by the traditions that decreed the nature of each garment, and by the fairy-tale castles perched upon mountain ledges. Indeed, John began to hatch on a new book of which Merano was to be the setting and the life of Otfried Mahler, a shoe-maker of Merano and of his wife, Ursel, the theme.

We spent some seven months in Merano and when at last we left it, it was to go to Florence, which neither of us had visited for fifteen years and which Evguenia had never seen at all. Our purpose was to see if we could not find suitable quarters for ourselves and for her in the following winter, and the manner of our going was sensational and will not soon, I think, be forgotten in Merano.

The train journey from Merano to Florence is vile, necessitating several uncomfortable changes, and we made up our minds to be extravagant and to travel by road. I expect that as usual I made calculations, that, on paper, reduced the extravagance to a minimum. But from one aspect of the journey there seemed to be no escape: the car did not exist that could accommodate the three of us, my dog, and all our possessions, nor did we feel inclined to

Una Troubridge in Florence. 1938.

Radclyffe Hall at work at 'The Forecastle', Rye, Sussex.

let our luggage travel alone. If the luggage went along with us we must hire two cars and the cost of hire would be doubled. But presently the garage proprietor had an inspiration . . . would the *forestieri* hire his motor-coach? True, it had seats for fifteen people, but the seats were easily removable.

So we left Merano on a lovely morning in a turquoise-blue charabanc of immense proportions; with John and I and Evguenia and my dog, Mary Rose on the seat behind the driver and mountains of luggage piled in the 'rumble' . . . Verona was thrilled, Bologna was delirious and almost mobbed us but Florence the cosmopolitan took us in her stride and barely noticed our passing.

Yet another dog this time: Mary Rose. She was a German, a little black and tan dwarf pinscher whom I bought in a Paris shop because she looked so frightened. She very soon stopped being frightened, however, and began a career of frightening other people. She bit the vet and she bit our cook, she attacked a nun and so many other people that she broke my nerve and I gave her to an elderly Italian countess, who admired her temper as evidence of devotion.

It was during this visit to Florence that we decided to make a home there, though at that time we had not considered parting with 'The Forecastle'. But I had loved Florence since my earliest youth; John had grown to love it almost as much as I did and she found its atmosphere congenial to her work. Also the doctors were unanimous in saying that the climate was sufficiently good for Evguenia and we hoped that she might be persuaded to stay there.

Moreover we had stepped into a circle of Italian friends who seemed to like us as much as we liked them. Partly owing to the fact that John's books, having been well translated, had earned her a very high literary fame in Italy, and partly owing to my being connected with an old Florentine family, the Tealdis, and through Aseanio Tealdi's wife, Sandra di Gropello, with other ancient Italian families, we passed at once through those gates that are usually closed to intimacy with *forestieri* and found ourselves made simply and warmly welcome in their houses and in their hearts. . . . We were all of one faith and looked at so many things in the same light.

Indeed, to this day, when I think of 'friends', apart from those at Smallhythe, it is chiefly of Sandra Tealdi, of May and Cencio Massola, of Maria Carolina Corsini, Elisa Imperiali, Fonfi Piccone and Elnyth Capponi that I think. And of how genuine and instant would have been their sympathy and understanding in John's last illness and in my bereavement. They are far away, as I write these words; I do not even know if they are all still living; thousands of miles of hideous war and devastation divide us, but I still feel that wherever they may be will be the nearest thing to home that I can expect to find on this earth.

When we reached Florence we stayed at first in hotels: the Albion and later the Gran Brettagna, and I distinguished myself by another attack of enteritis. . . . This at least gained us the friendship of that brilliant doctor and delightful person Professor Giglioli, who was so soon afterwards (so much too soon for all of us who loved him) to follow his lovely daughter Fiamma out of this world.

At first I was much handicapped in our hunt for a flat, but we kept our eyes and ears open and managed to inspect quite a number. John developed a craving for one that was exactly opposite our hotel but in this case I managed to head her off. Its entrance was in the Borgo San Jacopo and its charm lay in the fact that from some of its windows you could fish in the odorous Arno! But the rooms were small and dark and the only heating available was by minute iron stoves on legs known in Florence as *porcellini*. The owner, mistaking us for credulous tourists, assured us that it was never really cold in Florence. . . . I myself had more than a fancy for another apartment that actually boasted three rooms on the Ponte Vecchio. When we saw them chickens were being kept in the rooms and in any case they were small and very damp, but the address was almost irresistible!

At length we found what seemed to us ideal; a very sunny flat of the right dimensions on the Lung' Arno Acciaiuoli next door to Berchielli's Hotel. It was only a second floor, with not too many stairs and if its bedroom windows were on a narrow side-street, those of John's study and of my sitting-room opened on to one of the loveliest views in the world: the ancient houses of the Borgo San Jacopo with their feet in the water, while well in sight and a little to the left was the Ponte Vecchio itself and on summer evenings a great moon rising above it.

We have seen from those windows in that other-world clear light that precedes sunset in Italy, the procession of the Calcio, the football teams and their escort on horse and foot in sixteenth-century costume, leading the white ox with the gilded horns, pass by along the Lung'Arno, against a background of river and the Borgo San Jacopo. And we have also seen the modern horse artillery go by, all on white horses and sounding an uncannily melancholy and eerie fanfare on bugles hung with the pennant of the city, the red lily on a white ground . . . while we lived on the Lung' Arno we had no need to go to theatres or cinemas for our entertainment. . . .

We signed the lease of the Lung' Arno flat in the late

spring of 1936, just before leaving Florence for Paris and England. Our intention was to furnish it and move in as soon as we returned in the autumn.

But coming events were casting their shadows a long way before them and John, who had never been really robust, was never, to my mind, to know good health again. Already at Merano there had been signs of an affection of the eyelids that was increasingly to distress her as the years went by. It began as the faintest sensation of a foreign body in one eye but was actually a spasm of the lower lid which turned the lashes inwards against the eyeball and eventually affected both eyes to such a degree that she got little respite, work became impossible and operative interference essential.

Meanwhile, that summer while we were in Rye, what seemed at the time a trifling fall actually caused a triple fracture of her ankle. This was diagnosed by a local doctor as a sprain, allowed to set before an X-ray was taken, and when I removed her by ambulance to London the ankle had to be broken again and reset. We spent the remainder of the summer together in the London Clinic and when the time came for our return to Italy she was still on crutches with her ankle in a plaster case.

Moreover she was in a surprisingly weakened condition that did not seem sufficiently accounted for by her injury . . . it took her a whole year to recover completely, but at that time there were no symptoms to arouse suspicions of any sinister reason for her lack of recuperative power.

However, though weak in body she was never weak in spirit and she was utterly determined that whatever might be the difficulties, no illness of hers should be the cause of allowing Evguenia to face a northern winter. I therefore arranged for relays of carrying chairs, and we crossed the Channel with the assistance of a nurse who handed us over in Calais to another. In Paris we were delayed for just over a week: a mysterious inability to put her heel to the ground was discovered to be due to a shrinkage of the Achilles tendon which had apparently escaped the notice of her surgeon. A manipulator attached to the American Hospital asked for a month in which to put it right, but John, with her eye on the calendar and her mind on Evguenia, told him coldly that the most she could give him was a week. So at the cost of what he had warned her would be agonizing pain, the desired end was achieved and we resumed our journey.

Her weakness was extreme and when we arrived and our dear Giglioli hastened to our aid, there began an endless sequence of tonics and injections that seemed to have strangely little effect. Moreover, instead of making a rapid progression from crutches to a stick and from that to recovery, she practically had to learn to walk again and it was not until the following summer, on the evening before we left Florence, as we were wandering up the steep Costa san Giorgio that I remarked that her limp was entirely absent and she had at last left the accident behind her. I remember that walk so clearly; we stood and looked at Galileo's house . . . it was a very still, very hot night and as we came back home to the Via de'Bardi fireflies were floating along it here and there, enchanting little citizens of the City of Flowers.

But during the winter of 1936, when we were still staying at the Gran Brettagna, in spite of John's restricted activity, we were gradually furnishing and outfitting the flat. She was unable to revel, as she had hoped to do, in hunting and poking around with me for treasures, and this was a bitter disappointment to us both. But we did not do so badly, after all, and she was infinitely good and patient. . . . I

would discover the shops and would locate possible pur-
chases and then I would bring her along in a car or a
carriage. (Incidentally, the horses were so well supervised
by the Fascist government that even she was able to drive
behind them peacefully!) She could manage to walk well
enough inside the shops and if, more often than not, she felt
weak and exhausted, her indomitable spirit would bear her
up and we thoroughly enjoyed our bargain hunts together.

As regards the less interesting paraphernalia, I was
helped by a nice little Italian nurse, Signorina Bertet, whom
we christened Topolino, who knew the shops of Florence
inside out and piloted me in search of bedding, cutlery and
pots and pans.

All the same the winter was over and the spring upon us
before we were ready to move into our home. I know that
it must have been some time after Christmas, because of an
incident that has remained clearly in my mind. I had gone
out alone, shopping one afternoon, leaving John in the
hotel, as I thought, to rest. But when I returned and went
to our room I saw her sitting gazing fixedly at a small
object on the chest of drawers. She turned her head and
said triumphantly: 'Look, darling, I've got you your
Christmas present! . . .'

It was a little Madonna and Child of boxwood; an
exquisite early quattrocento carving of the Pisan school, and
she had placed it on a small mat of antique plum-coloured
velvet edged with gold. While I was out she had driven
with the nurse to the nearer end of the Via Guicciardini and
from there she had somehow managed to hobble on two
sticks along the narrow crowded street and in and out of
the Lord knows how many shops, seeking for some really
beautiful thing that would always afterwards remind me
of her love. . . .

The boxwood Madonna is still in Italy, somewhere, I believe, in that northern part of it now occupied by the Germans. May Massola took charge of her for me, together with a number of other treasures, when the world went mad in 1939. May my precious Madonna guard her and Cencio Massola in the terrible dangers that are now assailing them.

When at last the Lung' Arno flat was ready for occupation, I filled it with flowers and we took possession. I had secured a cook, an aged crone whose cooking was so superlatively good that we found ourselves overeating from sheer greed. Her appearance was an outrage to John's extreme fastidiousness; on occasions, when she had reluctantly to answer a bell, she would do so clad in a sacking apron whose front was glazed by the hours she spent pressed against the sink dissecting tiny sprouts and artichokes. Her grey hair hung in elf-locks and her manner to us was cringing, while she bullied her fellow-servant like a devil and even concocted an anonymous letter in a clumsy effort to get her dismissed. That fellow-servant was our dear Maria Prosperi, a young, round-faced Tuscan with innocent blue eyes, a crown of pale golden plaits and a lusty young body that kept on growing so that her skirts would persist in climbing above her knees. She was clever, willing and without guile: the only lie she ever told me was on the occasion of our first interview when she added on a year to her age, fearful that her youth might make her unacceptable. . . . The only time she ever showed temper was when, after she had stoically endured days and nights of agony, I discovered the truly terrible condition of her teeth and told her she must go at once to my dentist. Stamping her large foot she openly defied me; she would gladly do anything for Donna Una and the Signorina but she would not go and be murdered by any dentist; rather would she leave us, and at once, and before luncheon! I was very grave and deeply pained and the luncheon was watered by Maria's tears which dripped into the dishes as she handed them to us. When it was over I sent for her solemnly and she looked at me out of a face blistered with crying while I told her that she was a pretty young girl but could never expect to get a nice husband if she became disfigured by decayed teeth. . . . 'But, Donna Una,' was her desperate answer, 'how can I get there if I am too frightened to go?'

She served us devotedly, and so did Teresa, who later replaced our diabolical cordon bleu. Teresa thought that she knew how to cook. It was an illusion but we suffered it because of Teresa who was kind and honourable and pious, with a smooth black head that had never worn a hat, gold ear-rings and that ubiquitous Italian black dress with short sleeves. When she came to be interviewed she brought me roses, picked of course from the gardens of her current situation! When it became clear, in 1940, that our return to Italy would, to say the least of it, be delayed, they both offered to apply for daily work and to remain and guard our home without wages. . . .

But once again I have wandered up by-ways and have come a long distance from the spring of 1937 when we took possession of 18 Lung'Arno Acciaiuoli.

A flat had also been found for Evguenia: a furnished flat with which she was highly delighted. It certainly was charming, with views on a palace garden and attractive old furniture collected by the aristocratic but impecunious owner who had a real talent for house decoration. Evguenia's flat was also cool and airy; when she moved in we wondered if the heating would prove adequate; we had not then realized what we ourselves were to suffer. . . .

In March we revelled in our sunny flat. In April we talked much of the sunlessness of England. In May we lived lightly clad, in a penumbra of Venetian blinds and admitted that our bedrooms on the alley were stuffy and that sometimes we noticed unpleasant smells. But then, we also agreed that one couldn't expect to have everything, and what about the early mornings and the evenings, sitting in the study or in my 'salottino' with all the beauty of the earth before our eyes? In June we openly began to gasp and became alarmed: our lovely flat was incandescent . . . Moreover, with the coming of the 'warm' season, Berchielli's also began to suffer from the heat, and from every window opposite our bedrooms, apparently from sunset until early morning, hung American tourists exchanging their views on the beauties of Florence and their plans for further sightseeing. Nor was the river frontage any better, for there young Italy, also feeling the heat (it is a great mistake to think that Italians like hot weather) spent the nights in the open, leaning over the embankment, enlivening the conversation with occasional noisy quarrels or more often with excerpts from the more popular operas. Their voices were fine, though their ears were sometimes faulty, and despite the fact that they worked in the daytime, they all appeared able to dispense with sleep.

It was early July that brought the crisis; just about a week before we were due to leave Florence for the summer. One morning after an almost sleepless night, I went into John's room and found her sitting up in bed looking somehow as if she had straws in her hair. . . . She told me she hadn't been able to close an eye, that the noise and the smells and the heat were intolerable, that neither of us was getting any sleep to speak of, that if we went on in this manner we would be ill, that we had been imbeciles ever to take such a flat and that anyway her work was essential to her life and good work could never be done in such conditions.

She said all this and a great deal more while we eyed our breakfast trays distastefully in spite of the lovely yellow Cantagalli crockery. . . . I remember that that ubiquitous Italian sunshine was contriving to reach us even down the alley. I listened and agreed with all she said and she went on to tell me that when we returned in the autumn our first consideration must be to find another flat . . . and then quite suddenly, I went one better. I pointed out that if we waited until the autumn, we should be liable for the second year of our present tenancy and I announced that while she must lie down and try to get some rest, I would sally forth at once in search of better quarters. If I found a suitable flat we could sign the agreement, give notice to our Lung'Arno landlord before we left Florence and start life in our new abode in the autumn. She gave in after a few feeble protests, chiefly to the effect that flat hunting in such an atmosphere would kill me, and when she found that I was absolutely determined she announced her intention of coming with me. She said that no streets could be hotter than the flat. . . .

And so we set out together on that tropical morning, making a bee-line for the other side of the river where we might hope to find houses with a northerly aspect. I had rung up the agent Mr. Adams in the Via Romana and had received some addresses, but chiefly we relied upon walking along the streets we favoured and looking above the doors of the houses for the little card-board ticket that in Italy announced accommodation to let. Not only that, but if we liked the look of a particular house I did not hesitate to ring the bell and ask politely if this were not the house in which I had been told there was an empty flat available. But it was not until we had drawn a number of blanks and were very footsore and weary indeed, not until we had sadly decided that our energy was exhausted for the day, not until we were trailing homeward along the Via de' Bardi that the miracle happened: a little 'cartello' announcing: 'Luxurious second-floor apartment with loggia', at a moderate rent.

We signed the agreement for that flat next day. It was in a most beautiful trecento palace, it was all that our wildest dreams had hoped for, with large shady rooms and central heating and from its modest altitude on the second floor a long stairway led up to a magnificent loggia, open on three sides with views of all Florence from San Miniato to Fiesole and Monte Morello.

This time we had found a home indeed. There was a study for John such as she had never had before in all her life. . . . It was forty feet long by thirty feet wide, very lofty with a roof of carved chestnut and a cool red-tiled floor. It had not only central heating, but also a fine old hooded fireplace where in winter we could sit over a log fire. There was a curious little annexe or cell in one corner of the big room which had a radiator all to itself and in this she was to do most of her work – an austere little cell which we furnished with an oak table and chair, a big carved wood crucifix on the wall, and little else, and from the windows of study and cell alike one could look out on the Duomo, the Palazzo Vecchio, the Badia, the Bargello and Fiesole. . . .

And this flat had another feature that might have been designed for us. . . . Both our two communicating bedrooms opened through arched doorways into the big study, and if I woke in the night when John was working (and with the years she had become an inveterate night-worker) I could look from my bed right across the study into the cell and see her where she sat and reassure myself that she was all right and not in need of anything: of warmth or of food. . . . This was an immense advantage when her nocturnal habits became such that she would still be working at seven or eight o'clock in the morning.

Once or twice she walked into my bedroom at that hour and saying 'It's too late to go to bed now', announced her intention of going to Mass. But I soon put an end to that bright idea by replying that unless she went straight to bed I should leave mine and go for a walk in Florence in my pyjamas. . . . The trouble throughout her later years was that she really never got enough sleep. Not only had she always suffered from insomnia but after a night of intensive work – a stretch of perhaps sixteen hours on end during which she had reluctantly swallowed such food as I gave her, without leaving her desk – even when she finally almost fell into bed, within a couple of hours she would be wide awake, asking for her breakfast or going over her work. Often for four or five days and nights she would subject her system to this outrageous treatment and I sometimes pointed out that even her eyes could not be expected to endure being on duty for twenty or more hours out of the twenty-four, and that it was hardly surprising that they gave her trouble.

But since it was the only way in which she could work there was nothing for it but to make the best of a bad job, and this I generally succeeded in doing, though I should be sorry if I led anyone to think that I was invariably a model of patience and understanding! I shall not forget occasions when I told her that it was hell to live with her when a book was in progress, and I also remember saying that I did not know when she was more intolerable: when she was over-working or when she was unable to work!

In either case she would often reach a pitch of tension that was as painful to behold as it was to endure and at such times her irritability was extreme and so was her remorse when she felt she had victimized me!

Life with John was by no means always easy, but her variety was infinite and it was always interesting. If I knew discouragement, weariness and exasperation throughout the twenty-eight years that we were together I never knew boredom. . . . That is why life is so *dull* without her. That is why when at last her overtaxed body gave out and she could drive it no longer and she went to God for rest, I found that I had lost my occupation as well as my infinitely beloved companion.

For one thing she was the most simple of people, she was utterly without affectation of any kind. She was the most enchanting person to play with and *how* she could laugh! And how, also, she could make others laugh. . . . Subject though she was to accesses of deep depression, so often in these days when people speak to me of her, their memory seems to be of her laughter and recently Edy Craig said to me: 'I don't think anyone in the world has ever made me laugh as much as John did!' When we meet again, may there be laughter in heaven. . . .

Whether we played with our dogs or our birds (there was always a succession of rescued birds) or with our home or went out in search of amusement, she would throw herself into whatever we were doing with all the enthusiasm that she brought to her work. . . .

But latterly I would notice with a faint sensation of mis-giving that her pleasures were becoming increasingly vicarious. Generous and anxious to give pleasure she had always been. But during those later years in Florence I would sometimes comment to her uneasily upon the fact that she seldom seemed to covet anything for herself – that it was becoming more and more difficult to give her a present – and that the only thing that gave her real enjoyment appeared to be the organizing of enjoyment for others. Looking back on that time I think there was some instinct within me that told me she was loosening her hold on life.

But I am always thankful that we went to Florence, for so far as any place could give her happiness, and in spite of much anxiety that weighed her down and could not be averted, Florence and its beauty and the friends we made there were restful to her and suited her temperament.

She liked the exchange of simple entertainments and also the absence of any heavy drinking. She herself was moderate in everything but smoking and while she might occasionally celebrate with the best and was perfectly able to carry liquor, she hated what she called the alcoholic mentality that seemed unable to be convivial and sober.

Then she shared my adoration for Florence itself and on summer evenings we would walk and walk, exploring the network of ancient streets or we would drive up to Fiesole and dine with Isabel Graham-Smith and sit in her garden looking down on the city.

Siena she loved and San Gimignano. We went to Siena several times – once with Evguenia and once to show its beauties to a Russian friend of hers who had come to visit us and once we spent a week there alone together in the old Palazzo Ravizza that is so unlike an hotel. We visited that immense monastery of White Benedictines at Monte Oliveto. We attended Mass at Santa Caterina's house, kneeling upon the flags in the saint's little bedroom, and we discovered that curious old genius Joni, the finest copyist and faker of ancient pictures that Italy has ever produced. We climbed many stairs to his studio in an attic and found him concocting his '*imitationi*', which so many dealers have sold as genuine, one of them being said to have deceived even Berenson. A little old man like a dried walnut, grinding his own colours and preparing his panels and producing things of exquisite beauty. I bought John the head of a Botticelli angel which may be vainly sought for among the master's works, and we commissioned a copy of the Madonna and Child of Sano di Pietro in the Oratory of San Bernardino at Siena.

Then as a complete contrast we would go to Viareggio with its hideous gimcrack modernity, and be quite as happy there as we were in Siena or Florence. There was nothing to do and nothing to see except blue skies and the still bluer Tyrrhenian Sea. But the amazingly pure air was an unfailing restorative and we would walk, or drive for miles along the shoddy sea-front and come in hungry as hunters to superlatively good food. To hot fried *sparnocchi* fresh from the surf and other things almost as delectable . . . and then there was always the case full of books and we lay on our beds with wide open windows and I read aloud for hours on end and saw the tension fading from John's face and the sunburn making her eyes look blue, and blessed the hideous and tawdry Viareggio.

It was from Viareggio that we went one day to Lucca, but that was as late as the winter of 1938, when, for some cause that was still a mystery to us both, the air of Viareggio had not performed its miracle and John was patiently trying to conceal from me the fact of her continued and unaccountable weariness.

We drove to Lucca that day in a hired car and saw the cathedral and Ilaria del Caretto and we found and saw

Matteo Civitale's gentle and benevolent Madonna della Tosse. We bought gold medals of the Volto Santo and wondered rather hopelessly whether we should ever be able to muster the physical strength to join one of those gigantic pilgrimages that surge towards it four times yearly. . . .

And then I suddenly had an idea inspired by the confidence born of years of Tuscan courtesy. I obtained the address of the Metropolitano of the Cathedral and leaving John to rest in the car I went off alone to make my petition: was there any means by which a pilgrim, debarred by ill health from standing in crowds, could be allowed to see the Holy Face?

And behold, all the doors opened before me . . . Monsignore replied that so far as he was concerned he would gladly have shown us our Saviour immediately, but that quite apart from the question of its sanctity, the Volto Santo was the oldest wooden crucifix in the world, and when not on view was kept swathed in wrappings in order to preserve it from deterioration. He explained that it was the work of over three hours for two men to unwrap it and prepare it for exposition. But he hastened to add that we need only collect a few friends who would join us reverently in a private pilgrimage and at twenty-four hours notice he would uncover the Relic.

And so it happened that a few weeks later, John and I celebrated my birthday at Lucca, together with thirty-five friends from Florence who had eagerly accepted our invitation. We ourselves arrived overnight, with Sandra Tealdi, May Massola, Eliza Imperiali and Fonfi Piccone, all of them bound to us by ties of affection, all of them united to us in faith and anxious to join us in receiving Holy Communion at the shrine on the morning of the pilgrimage.

At noon the remainder of our guests arrived and after we had given them luncheon at the hotel we all made our way to San Martino to see the most wonderful Face in the world.

For those who are unfamiliar with the history of this great treasure, it may be explained that it is a carved cedar-wood crucifix of over lifesize, that has been in Lucca since the year 740. Historically nothing is known of its origins or of how it came there, but where history lapses legend takes its place. According to legend, the Volto Santo was carved in the Holy Land by Nicodemus; he who used to visit Our Lord by night. But it is also related that while he began the figure confidently, remembering clearly the be-loved features, when he sought to reproduce those features his skill failed him and he grieved until he fell into a sleep of exhaustion and despair. While he slept, however, other hands were working and when he awoke it was to see his Master's Face, carved by the angels for his consolation.

And indeed, when one beholds the Volto Santo, legend ceases to be hard to believe for only at Lucca perhaps in all the world can one truly understand why, when He spoke to men, they put down their nets and followed Him. . . .

I did not know, when I adored that splendour, that the day was not very far ahead when He would speak to me through utter bereavement and demand that I should tread the way of loneliness; but He knew it and perhaps it was for that reason that He gave me the memory of His Holy Face.

To Rome we went upon two occasions. The first time we took Evguenia with us for a deliberately planned orgy of sightseeing that ranged from the Tomb of Peter to the Foro Mussolini, from the Villa d'Este to the newly-built town of Aprilia on the Agro Pontino. John had spent many months in Rome with Ladye and knew it almost as

143

well as we both knew Florence. She was in her element acting as showman and guide, and though I shared her usual dislike of organized sightseeing, I also shared the pleasure she got on this occasion in giving us the benefit of her experience. She secured a car with a very pleasant chauffeur and it was quite amazing what she contrived to show us during the four days of our visit . . . even the meals were arranged so that we could sample the best food that Rome had to offer and John was jubilant at the success of her 'personally conducted tour'.

But the visit to Rome that was really fulfilling lasted only twenty-four hours and we were alone together. In May 1939 Professor Lapiccirella, who had become our doctor when our dear Giglioli died, had insisted upon an X-ray being taken of John's lungs, and the resulting pictures had confirmed his suspicions.

They revealed the history of her neglected childhood and although the scars upon them had long since healed he was very emphatic in his view that the damage was such that she should never again be exposed to the rigours of a northern winter.

I remember the arrival of those X-ray photographs. As John was just recovering from a sudden attack of fever, the good Topolino was in charge and was sent to fetch them. When she returned and John demanded her X-rays she seemed strangely embarrassed and unwilling to hand them over, saying that they should properly be given only to the doctor. John, however, insisted and had her way, and even her untrained eye could not fail to discern the curious patches and opacities that disfigured them. Characteristically she roared with laughter and pointing at the most obvious blemishes she exclaimed: 'I don't wonder you wanted to hide these, Topolino . . . either they aren't mine at all or else I've swallowed a trouser button!' Then she saw my face and humbly apologized for laughing.

But she stuck to her suspicions of a careless substitution and actually insisted upon another set of photographs which were merely a confirmation of the first. Although she continued to treat the matter lightly she yielded to my demand for a second opinion and it was for this purpose that we went again to Rome, to consult Professor Frugone, a most charming and brilliant doctor, quite young but already physician to the Duce, to Marconi and to other notabilities.

Of course I was anxious as we set out for Rome, but Lapiccirella, while inexorably of the opinion that her lungs were too badly damaged to be exposed to northern winters, had also been very emphatic that there was now no possible question of T.B. and that in that respect he considered her to be self-inoculated. We had realized at once that if Lapiccirella's view was confirmed it would entail our living permanently abroad (there could be no question for a writer of John's sporadic inspiration of regular migrations on a given date twice a year). But although she had at first rebelled at the idea of being what she called 'exiled', as soon as she had realized my distress and anxiety she had said quite quietly that she owed it to me after all our years together to spare me in every way possible and that if Frugone should agree with Lapiccirella she would put up no fight and would do as I wished.

In any case, when John was light-hearted it was almost impossible not to catch the infection and in spite of our problems we set out for Rome in a distinctly holiday mood. It was upon this occasion that we bought wine at Orvieto and emptied the flask by the time we reached our destination. We arrived in time for luncheon and went to the

Ambasciatori which proved expensive and not by any means good. Lapiccirella took us to Frugone during the afternoon and while the latter was as emphatic as Lapiccirella on the question of northern winters, he was equally re-assuring in his opinion that tuberculosis was a thing of the distant past and that no recurrence was to be feared. They were kind and efficient and treated John as the great artist that they knew her to be, and even she began to feel that although at times she was bound to be homesick, life in a country that held so many nice people would at any rate have plenty of compensations. So the remaining hours of our visit to Rome were very happy indeed.

We were up betimes next morning and sallied forth, fasting, for Mass in the crypt of St. Peter's. We prayed beside the tomb of Pius X and lingered by the ugly mausoleum of the dispossessed Stuarts and then we went out into the Piazza in search of breakfast. We found it in a café in full view of the great church, in the Via della Conciliazione, and we sat on the pavement in the early sunshine and devoured fresh rolls and butter and drank our coffee from tall wineglasses, heaped and brimming over with whipped cream. After breakfast we wandered in Rome and did no sightseeing at all; I remember we went up the Spanish Steps to an hotel just above them and decided that we liked the look of it and would stay there the next time we came to Rome! We lunched at Alfredo's and ate *fettucine* and were rather disappointed because, owing to our being early, the great Alfredo himself had not yet arrived and the *fettucine* as prepared by the head-waiter were just a shade below the usual standard. But we enjoyed our lunch and looked at John's photograph in the 'gallery of celebrities' on the restaurant walls, and presently our desultory pilgrimage was at an end and we were in the train on our way home to Florence. . . . That Roman visit is one of the good memories. . . .

Another expedition was undertaken later in that same year and had a double objective. We were due in any case to leave and re-enter the country in order to renew our right to the 'tourist lira' (an expedient suggested by the obliging manager of the Banco di Roma in Florence). Also, since by then there were rumours of war, we had naïvely decided to inspect Lugano as a possible place of refuge upon which we could rely and where we and the dog Fido could be joined in an emergency by Evguenia. She was by that time no longer in Italy but was living in Paris, visiting us only occasionally.

Fido was a very important consideration and one of our main objects was to ascertain beyond all doubt that in no event would he be refused hospitality. He was an outsize white poodle of unknown age and origins who had been bought by John in the Via Tornabuoni. On a December day of arctic *tramontana* she had seen him offered for sale in the street. He was closely shaven and trembling with cold and the transaction was a matter of only a few minutes. Half an hour later he was perfectly happy, sharing our luncheon in Doney's restaurant. He grew to love us both, but he was always her dog and he never for a moment allowed me to forget it; he was as clever as he was loving and as devoted as he was brilliantly intelligent. He became a very well-known figure in Florence, especially in Doney's tea rooms, where he would always sit upright on a chair beside John, occasionally laying one paw gently on the table until a waiter would bring two sponge fingers on a plate 'per il Signorino' . . . If he was kept waiting unduly he would get down from his chair and go to the counter and put both paws upon it in front of the glass bottle that held what he wanted. When war was declared Fido was in Paris boarded with the head keeper in the Bois de Boulogne; we had left him there, as we supposed, for the eight weeks of our intended visit to England, and there he had to remain for many months while at first we debated returning to Italy, and when that proved impossible, how to get him to England.

In April 1940 I wrote to Harold Stainton, for many years our vet and a valued friend, to ask if he knew of an enterprising young colleague who would fly to Paris and rescue Fido. His answer came promptly: 'I'm an old friend, aren't I? . . . What's wrong with me?'

Somehow he begged, borrowed or stole a dog box and got it accepted on board a plane and very soon afterwards we received a wire telling us that he and Fido had landed in England. And so Fido went through his quarantine and once more became our inseparable companion. He was growing old but he survived John by a year. It was actually almost a year to a day after her death that he made up his mind to go and find her; I do not think he had far to seek. . . .

But when we undertook our trip to Lugano, Fido was still young and lively and handsome though some people might have considered his appearance peculiar. With the onset of the summer heat we had shaved him all over with the exception of his head, his bracelets and the tassel at the end of his tail, and being very susceptible to sunburn he was covered with freckles large and small and looked like an enormous pink truffled galantine . . . he would be very shy at first after this operation but a few days would efface his self-consciousness and he would swing along beside John with his beautiful free action, looking up at her lovingly from time to time.

During the years of war when we heard of the devastation in northern Italy we often thought of that drive to Lugano through the beautiful, peaceful country . . . Bologna, Pavia, Parma and ugly Milano with its superb cathedral; the Villa d'Este at Bellaggio where we spent a night both on our outward and homeward journeys, John saying she wanted me to sample the finest hotel in all Italy. On the first occasion we arrived there in the breathless calm that precedes a summer storm. We stood on the balcony of our room and watched Como turn to the colour of steel, with two hawks hovering far overhead, and presently a rainbow. . . .

And that evening I remember that I read to John a book that filled us both with delight: *A Traveller in Time* by Alison Uttley. It had the genuine quality which John called 'other-worldy' and which appealed to her above all others. Fortunately I shared this taste to the full, and nearly all the books that we returned to again and again contained something of that element. Du Maurier's *Peter Ibbetson*, Hueffer's *Ladies Whose Bright Eyes*, Forrest Reid's *Uncle Stephen*, George MacDonald's *At the Back of the North Wind* and *Phantastes* were some of them and she loved also an early book of Margaret Irwin's: *Still she Wished for Company*. They seemed to fulfil something in her nature that was dissatisfied with material life; the something that would occasionally make her say that she was feeling happy because for the moment she had a sensation that the veil between this world and another was very tenuous indeed.

At Lugano we spent a night at the Splendide. We chuffed about the lake in the little steamer on the afternoon of our arrival, in and out of Italy at each little landing stage. Next morning we set out and explored the town, and going into an unassuming-looking church we discovered the great Luini fresco. We bought a Madonna of blue glazed majolica and a local book-seller recognized John and persuaded her to autograph copies of her books.

After luncheon we located a modest lakeside hotel which we thought would suit us in case of future need, but I remember that by that time John was terribly tired and remained in the car while I pursued investigations.

However, the frontier officials were charming about Fido and assured us that he would always be welcome and soon we were again at the Villa d'Este where rest and comfort awaited us.

The next day we ran straight through to Florence, only pausing to hear Mass in the Milano Cathedral. . . .

We were greeted on arrival by a beaming Maria, a Teresa wreathed in smiles and an almost delirious Fido. And that was the last excursion we were ever to make together in Italy.

There was a measure of uneasiness in our leaving Florence that summer. Rumours of impending war were still persistent, though Munich had partially drugged our commonsense and a scare in April which had put us on the verge of packing up had proved abortive. But, as Amerigo Antinori put it at Doney's Café: with a criminal lunatic in command of Germany we must all admit that anything might happen . . . except, of course, war between Italy and England. That was as entirely inconceivable as was John's particular bugbear: an alliance between England and the Godless Soviets. I remember a very happy luncheon party at Eliza Imperiali's where she became eloquent in her efforts to reassure John that such an alliance was for ever out of the question. Sandra Tealdi was there and May Massola and Fonfi Piccone and Mitzi di Gropello and her daughter Agnese, and the sun shone and we ate excellent Italian food and were united in our fear and dislike of the Germans and our conviction that the Axis would die of inanition. But nevertheless we were all of us uneasy and in our preparations for our summer trip to England there were conflicting elements of precaution and bravado. Lapiccirella was against our going at all; he thought the journey too exhausting for John and prescribed a summer spent in the Italian mountains. When he found that she was determined to go he told her severely that unless she was back by the tenth of October he would send the carabinieri to fetch her. At the moment of writing I do not even know whether Lapiccirella is alive or dead! We bought and paid for eight tons of anthracite to see us through the following winter and as we intended to be away only eight weeks we resolutely left the flat in full commission even to our clothes hanging in the wardrobes, telling the servants that all would thus be ready when a telegram should announce our return.

On the other hand I made a collection of a dozen or so very special treasures: the boxwood Madonna, the Joni pictures, Romaine's portrait of d'Annunzio, John's photographs of d'Annunzio with his dedications, the Duce's dedicated photograph, and several other things that we particularly prized and I put them together in a corner of the study and told Maria that if the worst should come (tears and cries of *'non lo dire, Donna Una!'*) she was to collect these things and put them in a taxi and take them at once to Baroness Massola.

We left Maria and Teresa and our home in July 1939 and that was the last time John was ever to see them.

With a pause in Paris to collect Evguenia, to see some of our friends and to put the beloved Fido in safe custody, we crossed the Channel together for the last of how many times, and we arrived at 'The Forecastle' on August 4th, having reluctantly decided that it must be sold, since we were going in future to live in Italy.

It must frankly be admitted that at that time I felt strongly that even if war should come, a woman of over fifty-nine and in John's precarious state of health could in no circumstances undertake any active war work and could serve her country to better purpose by preserving her life in a suitable climate and using the talents that God had given her. I was further influenced by a strictly secret panic at the mere idea of her being exposed to danger, and already there had been talk of hypothetical bombing, but I had more sense than to reveal such misgivings to John.

On the question of health I was, however, quite frank, and in this I had the wholehearted support of her doctor, who inquired whether she thought she would help her country by saddling it with an invalid liability. But this was later on, after that September day when we had sat in the little 'Forecastle' parlour and heard Neville Chamberlain make the fateful announcement, followed by the siren's banshee wailing. . . .

As I have already said, we had returned to England having made up our minds to sell 'The Forecastle'. It was out of the question to continue keeping up a house which would only be occasionally occupied during the summer, and while the circumstances of Evguenia's illness had already led to such a procedure for several years past, that had been regarded by both of us as a temporary measure. But now it was John's health that was in question, her unfitness for the northern winters being permanent, and we must harden our hearts and let 'The Forecastle' go.

In spite of our innate propensity for moving we found it a wrench to part with the cottage, even though we had become aware of its shortcomings. Unlike the Lung' Arno

Acciaiuoli flat, 'The Forecastle' was only habitable in summer. It was ruthlessly exposed to sun, wind and rain which engineered an alternate swelling and shrinkage so that its sixteenth-century plaster and timbers parted company. No amount of caulking would cope with this defect and we very soon found that in inclement weather we were driven from sitting in the parlour or study to seeking refuge in the dark little dining-room. All the same, the idea of selling it was definitely painful. John had given it to me and we had both adored it, and although that had been over five years ago we had actually been able to live in it so rarely that we had not had time to get tired of it. Nor was the situation improved by the fact that whenever our friends arrived to visit us they raved about the cottage and never ceased saying that there was nothing to compare with it in Rye.

Needless to say it quickly found a buyer and although he changed his mind and backed out when war was declared, in a very short time there was another applicant and 'The Forecastle' ceased to be ours.

The first alert, on the first morning of war . . . and we never knew whether it had sounded for a raid or whether it had been somebody's unpleasant manner of finding out whether Rye's A.R.P. was alive to its responsibilities. My principal memory is of Dodo Benson's valet, Charlie, hurrying to our door in full regalia of tin hat, gasproof suit and policeman's rattle, calling out: 'Miss Radclyffe Hall, Lady Troubridge, are you all right?' and of later drinking a glass of sherry with two young men acquaintances in a cottage up the lane and searching my heart as to whether I had been frightened.

And during those first few days of the war I certainly was frightened . . . *of being afraid* and, if I should have to be afraid for a long time, of being unable to hide my fear from John. It was not until about a week later when I had completely recovered my balance and was happily convinced that no one had suspected my trouble that John remarked quietly: 'You *have* been frightened, haven't you, my poor darling? I've been so terribly worried and sorry, but there was nothing I could do about it. You just had to get through it as best you could.'

But if that personal reaction was purely temporary there was another anxiety that never left me: what would be the consequences to John's health if, in spite of all the warnings we had received, she must not only run the risk of English winters but in circumstances that might preclude even normal precautions. Therefore, in spite of her considerable opposition, I began to concentrate upon a return to Italy and since she for her part was anxious with regard to the possible effects of the English climate upon Evguenia's lungs, she offered less resistance than would otherwise have been the case. It was partly for this reason that, 'The Forecastle' having been dismantled and being in any case, as I have stated, uninhabitable in winter, she agreed to make plans for a winter in the West Country, pending the possibility of returning to Florence.

At that time she was fully launched upon a new book and since the Channel coast was likely to involve many alerts and the doctor pointed out that shelters were unlikely to be salubrious, and since in those days we none of us suspected that we should never even see the inside of a shelter, we almost inevitably decided to go to Lynton. John and I had had happy times there in the past, riding and reading and walking with the dogs; it had the advantages of familiarity and the Cottage Hotel was also familiar.

So to the Cottage Hotel at Lynton we went, John and I

154

and Evguenia and our luggage, so tightly packed into a very moderate-sized car that it was almost impossible to move hand or foot, and our thoughts turned regretfully to the Merano charabanc. But in the autumn of 1939 England was taking the war more seriously than she did a little later when she almost began to doubt whether, after all, there really was a war, and we were lucky to get a car at all. So we squashed in, three abreast and tried to be considerate . . . at least John and I did, but on that occasion I remember that Evguenia was in one of her moods and was resenting the war as a personal insult.

In any case, Lynton was no place for her; a tiny village without any urban amenities, eighteen miles from the two nearest towns, it certainly lacked appeal for anyone who was not possessed of ample personal resources. For John, with work to do, and for me perennially engrossed in that work, for us both with our books and dogs and with horses available, Lynton and its beauty were sufficiently fulfilling. But for Evguenia who was in any case fretting for Paris, where she had had her own car and had led her own life among her Russian friends, who was essentially a 'town bird', half-hearted about riding and quite incapable of sustained reading for pleasure, Lynton must have seemed exile indeed.

The fact that its climatic conditions were the best available for her damaged lungs made very little appeal to her Slavonic temperament. Perhaps it was not altogether surprising that, as soon as she was able, she took her own line and departed to pastures more congenial; although I am bound to say that her doing so caused John very grave anxiety. But anxiety thrives upon imagination and it was not in Evguenia's nature to suffer more than momentary anxiety or to understand that she might cause it in others. As often before in their relationship, this complete dissimilarity of outlook was not conducive to John's happiness.

But in the autumn of 1939, some at any rate of our problems lay hidden in the future and here we were, crammed into a car, minus any animal for once in our lives (but that was a deficiency quickly remedied!), stopping at Salisbury for luncheon and to show Evguenia the cathedral and spending the night at the George Inn at Glastonbury where I remember the radio giving us hair-raising warnings of the 'secret weapons' threatened by Hitler.

Hitler . . . and now for a complete digression. As we sat and listened to his threats of total war, as we reflected upon what he had already done to Poland, our minds went back inevitably to the one occasion when we had actually seen him in person.

It was during the spring of 1938 when Mussolini brought him to Florence and such preparations were made for his reception as the Florentines are never likely to forget. From house to house across the narrow streets and across the façades of the ancient palaces were hung great swathes of evergreens studded with brightly-coloured fruits such as were beloved of Mantegna and Crivelli. Every house in the city, including our own, was supplied with silken flags, hand-painted and fringed, which displayed the devices of the city-guilds of Tuscany: dragons and tortoises, Lambs of God and geese mounted on velvet-covered halberds, hung beneath every window and formed a continuous archway across the Ponte Vecchio and the Por Santa Maria. And through this pageant of mediaeval beauty, standing beside him in a modern car driven at walking pace, through streets lined with angry Florentines who refused to applaud, in a silence that no coercion could exorcize, the Duce drove his honoured guest, Adolf Hitler. An unimpressive-looking little man with a nervous smile, he seemed sheepishly anxious to propitiate the Duce, who appeared to treat him rather cavalierly.

Did those silent Florentines feel in their bones that this man was something other than he seemed? Did an instinct tell them that he was Juggernaut and that tens of thousands of them and of their children would perish and their lovely land be utterly devastated in the name of that Axis which they hated and scorned?

But at Lynton in the autumn of 1939, the Axis was the last thing to enter into our calculations. Italy was neutral and if ever she ceased to be so would certainly, as in the last war, be fighting on our side. Winter was ahead, an English winter that had been strictly ruled out by competent doctors for both John and Evguenia. Winter, moreover, likely to be attended, if half the rumours one heard were true, by shortage of food and scarcity of fuel that would further intensify its dangers for the unfit.

All those latent fears of losing what I loved, all John's long-past predictions that she would die before me; all my dim but instinctive feeling that she was gravely menaced, rose up rampant within me to do battle with circumstances. If hell froze I was going to get her back to the south. . . . But I made, thank God, just one reservation: I prayed that my efforts should succeed only if it were God's will. . . .

In John herself I found no ally; she was very far indeed from wishing to leave England. Even though she was compelled to admit that physically she was entirely unfit for war-work of any kind, she repeated over and over again that one's place was in one's own country when that country was at war, that she couldn't go about labelled as unfit and that if she went away people would say she was skulking, and it was only by demanding the fulfilment of her promise to me and by emphasizing the risks incurred by Evguenia that I persuaded her to agree to my setting in motion enquiries as to how we might obtain permission to return to Florence.

At first it seemed as though permission would be obtained: persons domiciled abroad were allowed to return to their homes and financial facilities were granted to them. Our chief difficulties appeared to concern Evguenia, who, being a 'stateless alien' with only a Nansen passport, was subject to very much more stringent regulations than ourselves.

By the New Year, matters had become hectic and Lynton proved so inconveniently far from London that we made up our minds to move to Exeter, whither Evguenia had already preceded us. From Exeter we felt that it would not be too arduous to make occasional visits to London and climatically speaking there seemed little against it.

But it was in Exeter, only a few days after our arrival, that John went down with severe influenza . . . the first of a long succession of disasters that were only to end with her life on this earth. The influenza promptly attacked her chest and the very capable young doctor who had been recommended to me spoke gravely of 'damp patches' and of a possible X-ray. Moreover we found ourselves in the throes of one of the worst winters ever known in the West Country; every pipe in the hotel was frozen and the electricity, which was the only available heating in her bedroom, was turned off during several hours of each day.

When at last she crawled out on my arm into a pale, frost-bitten sunshine, even she had ceased to oppose my machinations and declared that if she was ever to work again she must do as I wished and get to a better climate.

There followed, as soon as she had gained some strength,

a series of trips to London where we stayed at the Rembrandt Hotel and wearily toiled from one building to another and in each building from one room to another, and sat in rows or stood in queues, trying to co-ordinate our permits and visas with those that were being granted to Evguenia. Overworked and under-staffed, the various officials were incredibly kind, and that kindness was due in many instances to the fact that they knew and admired John's work and were anxious to do what they could to help her.

By March we had very nearly achieved our purpose when suddenly and unexpectedly God spoke, with the voice of the Foreign Exchange Control of the Bank of England. At the time I did not welcome His utterance and did not realize that He had heard my prayers and had decided to save me from the consequences of getting my own way.

One day early in March we returned to our hotel to find a communication awaiting us to the effect that since we had been over six months in England we had ceased to be regarded as 'domiciled abroad' and must therefore give up any idea of being allowed financial facilities in Italy.

There was nothing to be done about it and as a matter of fact, John, who had not really recovered strength since her recent illness and who had found my determined activities very exhausting, heaved a sigh of relief at a development that released her from her promise to me and allowed her to remain in her own country throughout the war. . . . All the way back to Exeter and after we got there, she was very busy pointing out to me that the winter was over and that she had survived it; that the summer was before us and that for all we knew to the contrary the war might collapse before the coming of another winter.

We remained in Exeter for some little time, and from

there we made a series of excursions in South Devon in search of quarters suitable for the duration. In addition to our bedrooms John required a study, or at any rate a third room that could be used as such, and in addition to these we were looking for a place where there would be a Catholic church and where ponies would be available for riding.

Although we spent some really pleasant days pursuing our search (car hire being then still unlimited) we were not successful in finding our requirements and before very long we made up our minds that there was much to be said for the devil we knew and presently found ourselves once more back in Lynton. We went at first to the Imperial Hotel, having found the Cottage Hotel much changed from what it had been in the distant past. Moreover its approaches were via a steep hill and my heart had again been misbehaving, so that our Exeter doctor had stipulated that he would only consent to my going to Lynton if I avoided hills and got my exercise on a horse.

There is irony now in looking back upon the way in which John worried over that heart of mine; the restraining hand that was laid on my arm if I hurried upstairs or up a hill; the admonitions if I lifted weights; the insistence upon the doctor being sent for at the slightest sign of trouble, and upon my strict observance of his prescriptions... I can hear her voice, if I attempted to argue: 'Do you want to die and leave me alone?'

There was, however, one prescription that appealed equally to both of us. We had already, before our departure for Exeter, investigated the local livery stable from which we had been used to hiring ponies in the distant days of our earliest visits to Lynton. We had found it still flourishing and throughout the autumn we had ridden from time to time, but the hireling animals had aroused our compassion and their condition had much diminished our enjoyment. After our return we began to discuss the possibility of buying mounts for ourselves, or at any rate of hiring them for our exclusive use and ensuring that they should have what we considered proper food and care. Very soon an instance of callous brutality sent John raging out of the livery stable and led to the purchase of Tommy and Star.

Tommy was the butcher's pony. In fair weather and foul weather we had seen and heard him, swiftly trotting uphill and downhill, ridden by a boy with a gigantic basket who had little consideration for horseflesh. Tommy was un-diluted Exmoor, a light chestnut, small, shaggy and sturdy, and incurably addicted to that manner of action that is locally known as 'daisy cutting'. In other words he was quite incapable of lifting his feet and as soon as he was released from systematic over-work he stiffened and be-came so unsafe a ride that he had to go to the kennels.

But as soon as it was known that we wished to buy him he of course became the family pet; the butcher was very reluctant to sell and it required quite a large sum to per-suade him. Nor did Tommy meet his end until he had spent a happy year, bolting with John on the moor, trying to unseat her by a peculiar shrugging buck that was his own patent and finally lying down and trying to roll on me! Tommy, in fact, before John went rather tearfully to view his body and verify his demise, had really had a very good innings.

In the meantime she had given me Star and if Tommy was aged, Star was young, and she was also, just at first, mislead-ing. She was an elegant little animal, with some good blood in her, and was rising four when John bought her for me.

She was perfectly sound but had been so neglected by the farmer who offered her for sale that the vet, who on this occasion was consulted, was in some doubt as to whether she would survive. She had been left through the winter to run untended on the moor with at least fifteen feet of plough-chain round her neck in order to facilitate catching her. Her poor neck was not only wasted but galled, she was a living skeleton and she certainly could be considered a rescue. Moreover she had really lovely paces and though, owing as we thought to maltreatment, she was nervous of being handled, she seemed to be a perfectly quiet animal and suited, in John's careful estimation, to my inexperience. Star was the first horse I had ever possessed, and she was also to be the last. We kept her until our 'stable' had to go owing to scarcity of food. She recovered her stamina and grew fat and well and on a régime of excellent meals she also grew wilful and very lively. She never contrived to get me off, for as John would tell me, I must have been born with a capacity for sticking to a horse. But she, like Tommy, took to bolting on the moors and would buck in mid-gallop and indulge in her own particular brand of gigantic shying. Occasionally her behaviour was too much for John's nerves; she would make me dismount and insist on riding her and long afterwards, during her final illness, she remarked to me one day that the most unselfish thing she had ever done was to let me keep and ride that damned pony. . . .

Tommy had been replaced by a young mare, Morning. She was pretty, though ewe-necked and thoroughly tiresome. In fact she was so unreasonably nervous, so entirely unfitted for our peaceful purposes, that we eventually cut our losses and returned her to her former home and John settled down with Charles.

He was a bay, bob-tailed cob of uncertain age, rescued from another livery stable. A handsome little beast with a tremendous neck, he was reminiscent of Randolph Caldecott's pictures of the country parson on horseback. I thought his paces abominably uncomfortable, but John and he seemed to suit one another. She loved him and would spend happy hours in the stable grooming him and cleaning out his loose box. When I last heard of him a few months ago, he was alive, still flourishing, and taking jumps with a little boy up, at a country gymkhana.

Often, when the memory of those recent years which were leading me step by step to bereavement seems more than my lonely heart can bear, I conjure up pictures of John with the ponies.

Whatever she endured and was fated to suffer, those were good times for her and for me.

She had such a perfect seat on a horse; not sensational as was Cunninghame Graham's but beautifully secure and unselfconscious. And she had also the hands that are born and cannot be made.

Day after day we would set out together in good or bad weather, in sunshine or rain. Fortunately the horses, once acquired, had to be exercised and thus constituted an effective check upon her sedentary tendencies. Sometimes she would inveigh against the obligation. She would feel ill and tired; more than I knew, alas, and utterly disinclined for action.

But I would guiltily urge and persuade, laying the emphasis alternately upon our duty to the horses and my own pleasure in riding; never by any chance upon her need of open air and exercise. And presently, inevitably, her unselfishness would prevail and we would walk to the stables or I would bring round the ponies, trying not to see the

163

weariness and pallor of her face, disregarding her occasional accusations that my passion for riding was becoming a tyranny.

Wearily also, she would get into the saddle and in a silence of deep depression we would move off and then almost always I would have my reward . . . as we came to open country or to the Valley of Rocks and she met the pure air and the beauty that, as she would say, could only be seen from the back of a horse. As she felt the communion of horse and rider that never failed her to the very end (for she could ride when she was too weak to walk), she would breathe deeply and her weariness would fade. I can see her smiling at me over her shoulder, and very often indeed she would say: 'How glad I am that you made me come out; I'm feeling better now and simply loving our ride.'

And so we wandered all over the country, and the war and circumstances that had taken so much from her, so that her life was a tissue of physical prohibitions and disabilities, gave her back after many years one thing that she had really loved and which was doubly fulfilling in that we so completely shared it. Neither of us was bent on equestrian exploits; we were perfectly contented on our humble ponies, taking our own line and, as always, endlessly talking, coming home as soon as we felt tired or sometimes putting up the ponies at an hotel or a farm where decent meals could still be provided. (The feed for the horses we would take along with us, knowing that otherwise they would fare meanly or go fasting.)

Even when our own ponies had to be given away, sent into the Midlands to a farming friend who could be sure of feeding them, we hired local ponies and continued to ride. The last time was on October 28th, 1942, only five months before she was smitten down and the mysterious cause of her illness revealed.

That was a beautiful October day and we certainly made the best of it. We took with us the woman who ran the livery stable; she had known the countryside since she was born and was a very efficient guide. A lovely way she took us, unknown to us before, through swollen fords, and up and down steep declivities; a rough ride it was but beautiful beyond belief in the golden October sunshine. Eventually we came out on to the Moor and she exhibited the speed of her horse, which was home bred, and John's pony was stirred to emulation and made desperate efforts to race his rival until John almost fell off with laughing. At last, tired but happy, we made for home and as John dismounted she looked up and said, with her ready courtesy: 'Thank you, Dorothea, for that lovely ride, it's been one of the best I ever remember. . . .'

A good memory that, in bad times.

We did not remain long at the Imperial Hotel. It was by no means comfortable and its rowdy bar was obtrusive, not to mention its rowdy proprietors. Its chimneys smoked and its food went downhill and we were rather desperately contemplating our next move when Providence led us to 'The Wayside'.

Evguenia had not at that time joined us in Lynton, having preferred to remain in Exeter, but as rumours became insistent of a possible enemy invasion and of a consequent paralysis of transport, John began to feel that a stateless alien had better be close to her guarantors rather than risk possible isolation. She persuaded Evguenia, for the time being at any rate, to agree to taking a room in Lynton. And it was in the course of looking for this room that on a hot Sunday in June we called at 'The Wayside', spoke to Jack

Hancock who was working in the garden and later interviewed Marjorie Hancock in the friendly little sitting-room that was to be ours for over three years.

We were inspecting the rooms on Evguenia's behalf, but we took to our future landlady at sight and I am glad to think that the liking was reciprocal. When a few days later Evguenia decided upon another address I talked the matter over with John, who had been as favourably impressed as I had myself. She had liked the house and the rooms, she had liked the people, she was utterly sick of life in an hotel and moreover 'The Wayside' was close to the Catholic church. So I lost no time in asking Marjorie (as we very soon came to call her) whether they would take us 'for the duration', as their only permanent lodgers.

We arranged to take the sitting-room that we had liked so much, all the bedrooms and the bathroom on the first floor, and later, when we had really settled in, we took over the dining-room as well, so that John could use the sitting-room for working without being disturbed at mealtimes. . . .

Within a week we had moved in, lock, stock and barrel, and very soon we also began to move in the usual menagerie. The first to come was an African grey parrot which John had given me many years earlier. Partly owing to an incurable habit of screeching and partly because when we were chiefly out of England she had presented an insuperable problem, she had been given, under certain reservations, to our neighbour, that great parrot-fancier, the Duke of Bedford. Shortly before our move to 'The Wayside' it came to our knowledge that the Duke had also moved his aviaries and that 'Charlotte' was living in a heavily bombed area.

And so, on the day following our arrival at the Hancocks, John and I went into Barnstaple and returned in triumph with the first of the animals that they were to suffer so gladly. Charlotte had been neglected but she was well and loving and very soon as noisy as she had been in the past, and gradually it became a matter of routine for Marjorie to appear and remove the offender from the author's vicinity to the more hospitable kitchen. There countless wooden spoons were sacrificed as diversion and every sound that she uttered was approved. She has remained with the Hancocks in Lynton and the last time I handled her as I had been used to do she eyed me with chilly disfavour and nipped me.

That same month saw also the arrival of two dogs: a tiny red pekingese bitch which I appropriated and a King Charles spaniel of the same sex of which John grew very fond indeed. My peke was brilliant and Jane the spaniel was not. John said she suffered from delayed infantilism. She was gentle, she was good, she wished to be obliging, but her nerves had been shaken by bombing before she came to us and she was always finding herself at a disadvantage. Something or someone was always getting the better of her. To John, of course, her timid helplessness was irresistibly appealing and her love went out to the foolish, beautiful creature when she sat with her huge feathered feet splayed apart and gazed at her with anxious eyes full of a dim apprehension. John pandered patiently to all her peculiarities and when Jane, in spite of the most loving care, only survived her exactly one month I felt that John had probably fetched her, thinking it was best to remove her from a war-ridden world. She went before the advent of V weapons would have further shattered her poor little being.

And before very long, Fido emerged from quarantine and took his rightful place as a member of the household. He was given a tiny bedroom to himself and slept in the bed with his head on a pillow. At night he would regularly lay himself down on his side and wait for his blanket to be spread over him. Then he would raise his head as we kissed him in turn and then he would begin to snore with his eyes open as a gentle intimation that it was time for us to leave him.

At intervals, birds were added to the menagerie. A finger-tame canary that died in Bath: it was christened Pippin in memory of the canary of John's childhood. An immense and savage lemon-crested cockatoo which she bought at Harrods because it looked unhappy and was sufficiently sly to make a show of tameness. After it had refused to allow her to come near it and had borne down upon me like a vengeful vulture we found a good home for it with our vet at Taunton, whither it was escorted by both the Hancocks.

Horses and riding, dogs and birds, they are woven into the fabric of those years at Lynton as into that of all our years together, and I am very grateful to them, not only because we loved them but because their need for our ministrations helped to conceal the daily approach of an ominous shadow.

Looking backward during those hours of leisure that are now only too often mine, I sometimes wonder that I missed the writing on the wall; that, although from as far back as our later days in Italy John's health had in so many ways been failing, I, who knew her so well and should have been wiser, concentrated upon lesser ailments and remote possi-bilities, and was misled into attributing much to overwork and to that convenient formula: 'nervous exhaustion'. In common, it must be admitted with all the doctors who examined her, I never faced up to the fact that there must be some fundamental and sinister cause for the steady decline of her general condition.

So far were we both from any suspicion of the truth that

it was not unusual for her to say to me, if she saw me anxious or distressed about her ill health: 'Cheer up, darling, and don't worry; after all, you know, it isn't cancer!'

Of course there was plenty to lead us astray. She had never in her life been really robust and her methods of working would have told upon a giant of strength. The damaged condition of her lungs was incontestible; she had for many years suffered habitually from insomnia and while we were at Merano in 1936 the affection of her eyelids began to distress her. She was well aware that it was inevitably progressive and that when it should become quite intolerable only a very delicate double operation under local anaesthetic would, if successful, enable her to continue her work.

Added to all this both the Italian doctors attributed her exhaustion and extreme pallor to oversmoking and they were also dissatisfied with the condition of her heart. So, in May 1939, on their urgent advice, she took the cigarette she was smoking from her mouth and never lit another for nearly four years. As she utterly refused the assistance of sedatives this complete abrogation of an almost lifelong habit was in itself a terrific strain upon her and on many occasions I would find myself wondering whether the remedy was not worse than any risks involved. Moreover, she was already apprehensive about her eyes and for her the strain was greatly intensified by the fact that she had always chain-smoked as she worked and by her fears that even when she recovered her strength, and even if her eyes would permit of her working, her work would be handicapped by this enforced abstention . . . she had certainly begun her Pilgrimage of Grace.

But in spite of her heavy handicap she did quite a lot of work at Lynton. She went on with the book about the shoemaker of Merano, and when, after her death, it became my duty to destroy it, it was nearly half completed and I knew that I was burning some of her most beautiful work.

In spite of her eyes and her failing health, in spite of her unassuaged craving for the forbidden cigarettes, in spite of a thousand and one interruptions, worries and anxieties of all kinds, some of which were inevitable and some of which might have been spared her, she toiled on doggedly and what she wrote was good.

She even coped with her altered circumstances by entirely changing her whole methods of writing. A typist being unobtainable in Lynton, she took to making a careful copy by hand of her rough manuscript, a copy that was laboriously legible and well spelt . . . but luckily she was not forced to do so for long. I was not a trained typist and my speed was very limited and also I was nervous of my own incapacity, but I could not endure to see her labours doubled or to contemplate the additional strain to her eyes, and I volunteered to take her dictation.

I have always felt that some kindly saint must have taken pity upon our plight, for so far from my proving unsatisfactory, John, who had armed herself to exercise patience and forbearance, found my services perfectly suited to her needs. She certainly was both considerate and patient, but I for my part had long known all her requirements and we achieved an eminently workable combination.

For her it was at least some measure of respite from toil, for me it was the joy of being brought closer to her than ever before in the creative work that was an essential part of her being.

Immediately after her death I was besieged by the press with inquiries as to whether she had left any completed book or any work sufficiently advanced for publication.

On the impulse of the moment and much too unhappy to use my judgment I told the simple truth: that I had given her my promise that I would destroy the book upon which she had been engaged. Not unnaturally this statement led to a spate of press comment and it also procured me some tedious letters in which I was warned by a number of self-constituted advisers that I should be gravely wronging Radclyffe Hall's public if I took upon myself this act of vandalism. I answered a few of them and pointed out that such a decision had rested exclusively with the writer herself and that I had no alternative to that of honourably carrying out her wishes.

But there was one correspondent who had to receive a more detailed answer. This was an unknown member of the public who wrote assuming that the book was to be destroyed because Radclyffe Hall, having returned to the subject of sexual inversion, had in the end lacked the courage to permit publication. My reply made it abundantly clear that John had never been in any doubt that *The Well of Loneliness* contained all that she had to say on that subject; that she had never for a moment contemplated a sequel or any return to that aspect of nature, but that had she done so she would very certainly have published all that she had to say.

The true reason for the destruction of the book was a simple one: she had, during the closing years of her life, been very deeply hurt by someone and when she knew that her days were numbered she had forgiven both the injury and the person concerned. But she felt that into the writing of that book she had almost unconsciously allowed the intrusion of a measure of her personal suffering and natural resentment and, as she said when she told me to destroy it: 'It isn't forgivenesss if one leaves a record that might be recognized and give pain . . .'

I know she regretted the sacrifice of her work; no one knew better than she how good it was and no one knew better what it had cost her. But she was in no doubt as to what she wished; I gave her my promise, and after her death I lost no time in carrying out that promise.

It was very soon after we went to 'The Wayside' that the affection of her eyelids became so acute that work was at last an impossibility and we realized that something drastic must be done. It was not a condition that was in any way disfiguring but it was none the less distressing in the extreme: as I have already said, it was an involuntary spasm of the lower lids which brought the lashes in contact with the eyes and it was intensified when she looked downwards to write. Anyone who has suffered for even a few moments from the irritation caused by the presence of one detached lash in their eye will wonder as I did at the patience and courage with which for a number of years she endured the affection that I describe, resolutely making light of it and working against such a disability, while as resolutely facing up to the knowledge that the trouble must inevitably increase. At intervals I would remove the more obtrusive lashes and we also applied a succession of palliative treatments while fully aware that we were gradually losing ground.

When at last we had to admit defeat the Battle of Britain was at its climax and it seemed no moment to go to London for treatment and even less advisable should there be a question of operating . . . but having been warned of the delicacy of the operation in question we still clung desperately to faint hopes of some new alleviating treatment and we decided to consult an oculist in Bath of whom we had heard excellent reports. In Bath the climatic conditions would be favourable and at that time it was regarded as immune from bombing. And so, leaving Fido with his vet at Taunton and taking with us gentle Jane and Pippin the canary we set out hopefully for the Francis Hotel. In Bath were also two new friends, Lady Dorchester and Lady Radclyffe (the latter distantly connected with John by marriage, a connexion that both were happy to emphasize.) In view of the depressing object of our journey it was heartening to feel that they would be near at hand.

I do not propose to dwell at undue length upon the disasters that befell us in Bath, but in view of their far-reaching consequences, some account of them cannot be avoided. The oculist was young and reputedly a good surgeon. He spurned any suggestion of treatment, telling us definitely that unless the lids were operated ulceration of the eyes might ensue at any time, with consequent loss of sight. He described the proposed operation as so trifling that both lids could be done simultaneously and the patient return to Lynton within a fortnight. We had some misgivings, in view of the fact that others had spoken of this operation as serious. But after all, we were eager to believe him and John was desperately anxious to get back to work; moreover even she could no longer endure her condition.

Kathy Dorchester volunteered to look after Jane, and a couple of days later we went into a nursing home, retaining our room at the Francis Hotel to which the surgeon had told us we could return in a few days, as soon as he removed his stitches.

It had been decided at John's desire that the eyes should be done separately at a five days' interval: she said she preferred to keep one eye in use! But six weeks elapsed before the second eye could be done, the surgeon having caused so severe a haemorrhage that a subsidiary operation was required to disperse it.

Over the second eye he had apparently lost his nerve; he cut too close to the roots of the lashes, causing subsequent eccentric growth which, when his operation broke down soon afterwards, actually intensified the original trouble.

John was to endure that particular misery throughout the remaining days of her life. Although, after two other eminent surgeons had refused, Sir Harold Gillies agreed, though reluctantly, to remedy the condition, she was never again considered well enough to undergo the ordeal of what he warned us might prove to be more than one operation.

But John being what she was, even that grim time at Bath has memories the reverse of painful. After all, we were together, actually sharing a room and never separated, except when, once a day, I went to the Francis Hotel to feed Pippin. Our friends kept that room filled with beautiful flowers; as usual we read much and talked endlessly and during John's convalescence there were several days that stand out as being good to remember. One was the morning when, with our two friends, we visited the Baths and had coffee and biscuits in the summer sunshine, sitting by the edge of the warm Roman bath, and another was the expedition we made, taking John's nurse with us, to Downside, where Dom Thomas Symons was waiting to greet us, and to show us all the beauties and treasures of the Abbey. He played a Bach fugue for us superbly in the empty church and later gave us tea in the Abbot's parlour, which had been lent to him for the occasion. And although I was nervous lest John should get overtired, her admiration and enjoyment were so sustaining that she was all the better for the effort.

Our common love of our Church, of its ritual, and of religious art and literature, was always a very strong bond

174

between us. John was actually more consistent than I was in observances but fundamentally I do not think I was less fervent. One of the attractions of 'The Wayside' had been its close proximity to the Poor Clare Convent and Church, where two Abbesses in succession were John's devoted friends, to whom, through the intervening grille, we would pay frequent visits. Mother Marie de l'Ange Gardien went on to prepare a place for John, just over a year ahead of her. Mother Mary Clara is still my treasured friend; we correspond regularly and if I should eventually live in Italy she is one of the few people who will always, at intervals, bring me back to England.

But that disastrous experience in Bath, bad as it was, was only, had we known it, the beginning of our troubles. It was in December, after our return to Lynton, that I, who was still giving daily treatment to John's eyelids, had at last to admit to myself that all was not well, that something, in fact, was very wrong indeed, and had to tell her that what she had endured had to all intents and purposes been in vain.

The operation on the right eyelid had definitely broken down, and after another highly unsatisfactory visit to Bath, we at least had the sense not to consent to further experiments and decided that, blitz or no blitz, our only course was to go to London and obtain the best opinions available.

It was within a week of our arrival at the Rembrandt Hotel and in mid-December of 1940 that John developed what at first seemed a mild attack of influenza and it was in the course of that arctic winter, when London's streets were sheeted with ice and snow, that all the gloomy predictions of the Italian doctors were fulfilled. Bronchitis developed and was followed by pleurisy and these were presently joined by double pneumonia, and for seventeen weeks I fought for her life, with her own gallant assistance as soon as she was conscious enough to give it. Young and active nurses were by then unobtainable and I had to make do with elderly women who made no pretence of being adequate for so serious a case.

She lay long between life and death but she rallied and somehow she managed to crawl back to life, though one doctor who was young and another who was old (we had not then met Doctor Armando Child who was to be such a tower of skill and kindness later), both contrived to miss the true significance of certain symptoms that to quicker brains would have been all too enlightening . . . and we were still together, and when I drove her back triumphantly to Lynton, weak and emaciated but with the summer ahead of us, and stopping, of course, to collect Fido on the way, we had acquired a certain measure of confidence that we had met and overcome the worst that could befall us.

I was to exercise increasing care and vigilance; Marjorie was to prepare good and nourishing food and John was to display courage and patience in a life that seemed chiefly made up of restrictions: she was not to work for some time, she was not to smoke, she was not to leave the house in rainy or windy weather (which in England meant, as Elizabeth Barrett knew so well, confinement to the house for weeks on end), she was not to do this, she must never do that, she who had been incarnate activity, and provided she followed this dreary mode of life she might hope to go to London again in six months' time and to be allowed to have her eyelid re-operated . . . Meanwhile that same eyelid gave her little peace and she had to endure it as best she might, relying on me for the frequent extraction of lashes. Life had indeed taken most things from her, and she also had other very grave anxieties. And yet, when I talk to Marjorie Hancock who lived in the house with her through all that time, it is John's laughter that she, like Edy Craig, so often seems to remember, and again and again she will end some reminiscence by saying: 'Do you remember how she used to laugh? ...'

When she could not use her eyes for work she took to knitting because it kept her hands occupied and did not involve looking downwards. And to that also she brought the painstaking perseverance that had become so characteristic of all that she did. Even in such a trivial occupation, nothing but perfection was good enough to please her, and I possess scarves and fancy blankets which she knitted for me of which the neatness and regularity are enduring evidence of her patience. And always while she knitted I would as usual read to her. Among other books I read her everything I could get hold of that dealt in any way with the life of the Brownings. Apart from our common love of their works we had always been interested in them as personalities, and in Florence, where they had lived and loved so near to our home this interest grew to be an active affection such as we might have felt for them as living friends. We would walk along the Via Maggio to Casa Guidi and stand looking up at the marble tablet that bears testimony to their love and to his enduring sorrow, and just before we finally left Florence we had even gone into the palace and looked up the staircase. As we read of the peace and beauty of their life together John evolved the idea that after the war, if and when we returned to Italy, we would try to obtain a lease of their apartment. She would say thoughtfully: 'I think I should like to work in the rooms where Robert and Ba were so happy together. ....

As the spring advanced her life became slightly less restricted; we could ride and she would sometimes work in the little garden, but almost we began to believe in some

177

fatality when one morning in early summer as she was leaving the house for a walk with the dogs, she slipped on the doorstep and cracked her ankle, which had to be in plaster of Paris for nearly six weeks.

This time she hobbled around on a 'spur' but her mysterious weakness made such efforts distressing both to herself and to me and we decided to employ this period of renewed inactivity by fulfilling our 'medical' engagements in London.

Our stay was a brief one and without salient features, except that she paid some painful visits to the dentist. We were told that her lungs had escaped further damage, that she might, if she wished, smoke four cigarettes a day and a very eminent consultant indeed, after what was at any rate a lengthy examination, informed her that apart from her lungs needing care there was physically nothing of any kind wrong with her that could prevent her becoming perfectly well. . . .

But in spite of this encouraging pronouncement, she was nevertheless very far from well and no one seemed prepared to pass her as fit enough to have her eyelid operated on. We were told that further delay would be advisable and presently we returned by ambulance to Lynton as ignorant as we had been before our visit of any condition that might account for the fact that so healthy a woman was steadily losing weight and was suffering from recurrent attacks of exhaustion and weakness that made her sometimes almost unable to leave her bed.

But her courage and her nervous vitality were great and the summer weather was always her ally. The ankle was repaired and though it was none too good for walking it did its duty when she was on a horse. Moreover, having been told that she ought to be well, she was determined to do her best to be so, both because of her desire to reassure me and because of her literal horror of letting her nerves master her. . . . If her body was, as she had been told, in a relatively sound condition, then it could only be nerves that made her feel so ill and to these she had no intention of giving way.

Her voice would be full of shamed apology on certain mornings when I went to her room and her eyes would look anxiously at me from her thin, colourless face as she asked me whether it would give too much trouble in the house and whether I thought she would be giving way if she spent a part of the day in bed. In spite of my eager assurances that she needed rest, she would generally change her mind after her breakfast and drag herself through the process of dressing. She carefully maintained her almost phenomenal neatness, and once I remember, as I sat there watching her weariness, I found that the tears were running down my cheeks.

She saw them and exclaimed in distress: 'Darling, tell me, what's the matter!' and all I could answer was: 'It's you, *you*! . . . They say you should be well and I take such care of you and I do get good food, and yet you look so ill and you keep on getting thinner and thinner. . . .'

And she answered: 'You know it's only nervous exhaustion. I'm working again and I'm never well when I work. . . .' But a moment afterwards she added thoughtfully: 'But I do feel ill, these days: sometimes I feel better than others, but I practically never feel perfectly well. . . .'

It was true she was working on our return from London, in spite of her eyes and in spite of her weariness, and in spite of this mysterious feeling of illness. Since she had been told that she had made a good recovery she admitted of no reason for being idle. If I cared (which I do not) to indulge

179

in retrospective bitterness, I could feel very bitter indeed about that professional ignorance that took from her, during the last year of her life, the right to cease driving her failing body, to take with peace of mind and self-respect the rest she so sorely needed. There were times when some passing ailment would keep her in bed and when she would look at me with a smile of self-mockery and say: 'I'm so glad to feel that I have a right to be ill! I'm really not allowed to get up now, am I?'

But equally mysteriously, as it seems to me now that I myself am no longer ignorant, there were days when she felt surprisingly strong; when she worked with a will and I took her dictation knowing, as she did herself, that the work was good. When, as I have said, we galloped across the moors and her face would lose the expression that I dreaded and that I now so often saw in her unguarded moments: that growing expression of patient resignation.

There is a picture that often rises in my mind, a happy picture in which I find comfort, that I sometimes saw from the window at 'The Wayside', and that dates from those last months before we left Lynton. I see her in breeches or jodphurs and a béret, swinging along towards the house from the stables, pausing at intervals to crack her crop, childishly pleased at the noise she was making and looking up as she came nearer to see if I was watching her and appreciative of her prowess. . . .

She would get up early and we would go to Mass together, at the beautiful little church across the way, or if I was too lazy to turn out betimes she would go alone and I would be at the door of the house awaiting her return and we would breakfast together in the friendly little room that had become so much our own in more than three years. Indeed, thanks to the Hancocks we had taken complete possession and its walls were hung with portraits of John's forebears and with miniatures and silhouettes which had been brought from Rye to save them from the bombing.

While as for books, as always I seemed to breed them. Latterly there were three bookcases in the sitting-room and others sprang up all over the house and occasionally John would make a mild attempt to put a check upon my inveterate bibliomania. She herself was entirely without that sense and always maintained that she cared less than nothing whether a book was worth sixty pounds or sixpence provided it was printed in readable type. But she was wonderfully indulgent to my contrary view, and our library of some four thousand volumes was largely the outcome of this generosity. It was characteristic of her too that towards the end, when she was desperately ill and I was sitting beside her bed, she said in a voice that was barely audible: 'All the books you want now, darling ... you may get them all. ...'

And now I have finished writing John's life and the time has come for me to write her death, and if she always met life with unfailing courage she also accepted death with perfect faith and trust in the wisdom and mercy of God. And she accepted it with open eyes in one of the most terrible forms that can destroy the poor terrestrial body, for, to borrow a sentence of her own from that last book that I burned: she wished to be worthy of the fellowship of death.

Months after she was taken ill Doctor Child said to me in wonder: 'Isn't she afraid? Surely she must be afraid ... everyone is with cancer ... but she never seems to think about it at all and I've never seen her show a sign of fear.'

If she did sometimes feel afraid, knowing so clearly from the first what awaited her (and being human her courage must sometimes have faltered), she managed to hide that fear so successfully that even to me, her other self, in all the months during which I never left her side night or day, she never allowed it to be perceptible. It was not within the power of her love to spare me her suffering, but at least she could spare me the knowledge of her fear.

This is not a medical or surgical treatise and I am not proposing to harrow those who will read it with a grim record of the sufferings of those last seven months. She endured them and they are over and she can never suffer again, and I survived the special anguish that is reserved for those who must learn that upon this earth love can be utterly helpless and powerless to protect. But what I do earnestly wish to relate is the manner in which, as her body weakened, her splendid spirit gathered unto itself beauty and strength until the earthly vessel that held it broke and it winged its way straight to God who made it.

I wonder whether I, who am unskilled in writing, can ever find words to describe, even dimly, that strange and fulfilling happiness that blossomed for us as we knelt together in the Garden of Gethesemane.

It is true that, being still clothed in human flesh, we could not always hold on to that happiness, and of that John's wisdom was quick to warn me, foreseeing that in the long days ahead there would be hours when darkness would cover the earth. 'One cannot always remain on the peaks,' was how she put it, 'we shall sometimes have to go down into the valleys.' But even I who must wait in loneliness have learned for my sustaining that there is no joy on earth that can compare with that which is the child of love and sorrow and which is the pledge of the perfect joy that is to come.

It was towards the end of March 1943 that she was suddenly taken acutely ill. Of the three weeks of mismanagement and avoidable suffering that followed before I took her to London, it suffices to say that local talent diagnosed her illness as a severe chill and local talent being suspicious of Popish practices, a consultation led to the pronouncement that the chill was due to her habit of going fasting to early mass.

For the first ten days I nursed her myself with occasional assistance from the district nurse, and it was John herself who then raised a protest: I could not continue nursing her by day, snatching sleep at night on the edge of her bed, seeing to the catering and taking care of the dogs, and I must lose no time in getting a nurse. And in this respect I was fortunate indeed. It was quite impossible to get anyone locally and the first address that came under my hand was that of a vaguely remembered little nurse who had once looked after John at the London Clinic for twenty-four hours after the extraction of a tooth. We both remembered that we had liked her personally, but we knew less than nothing of her professional qualifications. However, as we were told that John's condition, though so painful, was not serious, I wired to Nurse Baldwin and she duly arrived. She had been working very hard at a London hospital and her husband had urged her to consider her health and to accept an easier case in the country!

Nurse Baldwin was all that a nurse should be and her presence brought comfort to my growing panic and when, a few days after her arrival, local talent quite suddenly confessed misgivings and I made a lightning resolve to get John to London, it was Nurse Baldwin's resourcefulness and ready acceptance of responsibility that enabled us to accomplish that terrible journey.

She nursed John with selfless devotion for months, being present at both her operations. She was human and light-hearted and had a sense of humour for which John herself would often thank God, saying that 'little B', as she very soon christened her, had helped her through many bad moments. And when after several months 'little B' was compelled to rest, she persuaded her equally efficient sister to take her place and they were both with us at the end.

One of the major problems in getting John to London was what seemed at first the utter impossibility of finding any hospital or nursing home that would not separate us. Accustomed for years past to the ways of France and Italy (John told me they were also those of America) which recognize that in cases of grievous illness affection may play a valuable part in recovery and, therefore provide accommodation for a patient's friend or relation, I spent an entire desperate morning on the telephone meeting with refusal from every direction as soon as I explained that if they took the patient they must be prepared to supply me also with some kind of accommodation. Vainly I pleaded that I did not require a room . . . that a sofa or cot in any corner would suffice, that I was willing and able to spend the nights in a chair, but finally I was told by one of the hospitals that if I chose to spend them in the waiting-room there was nothing that they could do to prevent me. I humbly and thankfully accepted this concession, for although the local doctor assured me that there was no hurry, both Nurse Baldwin and myself knew that such was not the case, and I ran up to tell John that everything was arranged. I had barely done so when the telephone rang; the hospital had thought it over and had repented its weakness; unless the patient was in urgent danger, I should not be allowed to spend the night in the building.

It was impossible to keep this impasse from John, who took up her stand with the utmost determination. She would do as she was told in all but one respect: if she died where she was, she would not be separated from me, especially in London and at a time when there were possibilities of bombing. And as in this respect I entirely agreed with her I gave her my promise that whatever happened we should remain together and I returned once more to the telephone.

It was Doctor Child who came to my rescue. He had quickly gathered from my answers to his questions what was likely to be discovered on our arrival. He told me to bring John up to the Ritz, promising to be there to meet us and in the meantime to communicate with a surgeon and to find accommodation for us both.

There followed the wartime difficulty of getting an ambulance, but forty-eight hours later, after a nightmare journey of over two hundred miles, Cecil Joll and Armando Child had examined her at the Ritz and had left the room to discuss their course of action.

It was then, when we were alone together for a moment that John looked at me with pitiful eyes and took command of the situation. She said. 'You know, don't you, that this is probably cancer? And if it is, that it's God's will and that it must not only be accepted but welcomed?'

I cannot remember what I said in reply; I know that I did not fail myself or her. She had nailed the colours of her faith and mine to the mast and there she kept them while there was breath in her body.

When Cecil Joll and Armando Child returned she demanded the exact truth regarding her condition and was told it and next morning, hearing that Mickie Jacob had called, she insisted upon seeing her and asked her to look after me if she herself should not survive the impending operation. When Mickie had promised and had left us, John laughed: 'Did you see old Mike weeping her eyeglass out of her eye!'

That afternoon we went down to Lady Carnarvon's home in Hadley Wood and that evening Cecil Joll operated . . . as I know now, her case was hopeless from the first, but measures were taken that just possibly might have prolonged her life for several years. At the time this hope was the one faint gleam of light for me in a bottomless pit of horror and despair.

As soon as she had come out of the anaesthetic sufficiently to recognize me and to know that I was near her they gave her morphia and sent me to my adjoining room. But although little B had gone off duty, completely exhausted, she had been wise before she left her patient and had warned the night nurse of what was likely to happen. In my absence the morphia failed to take effect and before long I was told that she kept asking for me and would not rest unless I came to her.

I think she would have slipped away that night if I had not sat beside her and held her hand till morning; every time she opened her eyes she saw my face, knew that I was there and drifted back to sleep. In the morning they told me that she would live.

Many times afterwards I wondered whether it would not have been less selfish to let her go then in peace, but at other times I know that I acted as I did for her good as well as mine and in order that to us both the glory of God might be made manifest.

Lady Carnarvon's home was then in its decline and John was actually its last patient; Lady Carnarvon herself was kind, but the organization had gone to pieces and its nursing and discipline were non-existent.

But perhaps it is because of that very fact that I am able to look back upon it with a measure of gratitude, because in no other nursing home could we have been so completely independent.

We had our own day and night nurses, of course, and during the two months of our stay we were never apart save for a quarter of an hour daily when I walked in the garden or the near-by woods for exercise. From early morning until evening I never left John and though there was a bed in a communicating room I never once used it but slept beside her on two armchairs so that every time she awoke in the night she knew that we were still together.

This strange joy and peace that had come to us in pain and sorrow was so precious that we could not bear to lose a moment of it, and indeed during the six and a half months of her illness I continued to be with her always night and day. On the very few occasions when for unavoidable causes I left her for as much as an hour, she fretted for my return and once, later on, at the London Clinic, when I had a slight attack of influenza and a tactless sister suggested to her that I might be sent out of the building, weak as she then was she sent for the matron and expressed her indignation so forcibly that during the four days of my isolation I was given a room not far from her own.

Within a very few days of her two operations (a second one had been necessary which she had hardly been expected to survive) she knew all there was to know about her own condition. I had been told that so long as her extreme weakness continued I was not to reveal its full implications, but I had never yet lied to her in my life and when she questioned me closely I replied only by evasions or a revealing silence. Armando Child came to see her every day and already his admiration of her as an artist had merged into admiration of her character and of her courage; his gentle soul shrank from the task that he knew awaited him as soon as she was strong enough to demand the truth.

But he need not have feared. Had he known her better he

would also have known that well or ill it was not her habit to lay burdens upon other shoulders. A morning came very soon when, with a weak flash of humour, she observed: 'I call it a shame; you've been left holding the baby! Do stop swivelling your eyes and wondering how to tell me I've got inoperable cancer . . . of course I know it quite as well as you do. . . .'

I was perfectly frank with her so far as my own knowledge permitted. I had been told by the surgeon that there was reason to believe that she might regain a measure of health, resume her work and live for several years. He also told me (doubtless a merciful lie) that it was unlikely that she would suffer pain, and that the end when it came would be merely wasting and an increasing weakness. Such was the extremity of my grief and fear for her that I literally flew to her with this prognosis. My sense of humour was definitely in eclipse but hers was by no means dormant.

'Will you listen to Una, little B!' she exclaimed, hardly able to speak for laughing. 'You would think she had brought me the most wonderful news, and what it really boils down to is that I shan't die in agony but only fade away and die of weakness. . . .'

Friends wrote to me suggesting various forms of treatment which they urged should be undertaken without delay, but together we looked the thing clearly in the face and while she left the decision to me and was willing to undergo anything if it would give me comfort, neither of us had any confidence in these desperate expedients and we were very soon perfectly agreed that we would not waste such time as might remain to us, chasing after forlorn hopes that were unlikely to be fulfilled.

For herself she had no fear of death and no desire to live and I realize now, as I refused to do at the time, the horror with which she personally envisaged a life such as would, at the best, have been hers. A life of complete invalidism in conditions repugnant to her in every way and with inevitable decline and a possibly agonizing death beyond it. For my sake and because she hated to leave me, she accepted this prospect with unfailing cheerfulness, but sometimes she would look at me and say: 'It's only for your sake that I want to live, I want to go on taking care of you and not to leave you alone', and when, at times, the flame burnt very low, she would whisper: 'I *am* putting up a good fight, it's entirely for your sake, and I shall go on fighting....'

When she was asleep I would sit beside her, desperately seeking comfort and making calculations: neither of us was young; we were, in fact, ageing . . . separation on earth was the universal lot unless people had the amazing luck to die or be killed together. . . . Miracles did happen. . . . How old would I be if she lived for five years, for ten years, for fifteen years? For how long must I expect to have to survive her?

Sympathetic friends produced a gallery of cases that were well and active after twenty-five years. . . . I read those letters again and again and used them to drug my increasing realization that she was slowly but steadily losing ground.

From the Carnarvon Home to London, to a home in Primrose Hill where even she rebelled at the gloomy surroundings, but it seemed to be the only place available to us both. And then, by luck, a vacancy occurred at the London Clinic. It was what was technically called a 'suite', one room divided in two by sliding doors with a divan upon which I was allowed to sleep, when I did not prefer the chair at her bedside. There again, thank God, they were understaffed and realizing that I relieved them of much of the nursing and that I also always retained two special nurses, they let us pursue our way without much interference.

And finally, when everyone but myself knew that the end was at hand, when John, if I left the room, would look at the nurse and say desperately: 'Is no one going to tell Lady Troubridge that I'm dying?' While Armando Child tried tactfully to prepare me and I replied that the surgeon continued to predict a partial recovery, I moved her to a furnished flat in Dolphin Square.

Pain had come, as everyone but myself had known it was bound to do. And with it had come a deathly sickness that was not less wearing. But she met them with a courage that seemed to increase with her bodily weakness, and if she had been good to look at when in health, she now had a beauty that was almost unearthly. As she lay sometimes, asleep at last, I would sit and gaze at her wasted face which seemed as though it were carved out of ivory in its clear pallor and its exquisite purity of line and plane.

The day before she died, in the throes of suffering that we were powerless to alleviate, she looked up at the nurse with a ghost of her old, jaunty smile and murmured: 'What a life!' but a moment later she looked at me with her eyes full of courage, threw back her head and added: 'But I offer it to God. . . .'

She had always believed that I would survive her and after her death I found that she had written me a letter and in it she said:

'God keep you until we meet again . . . and believe in my love, which is much, much stronger than mere death. . . .'